ETHICAL PROFIT

A Guide to Increasing Profit
Using Sustainable Business Practices

Samantha Richardson

First paperback edition January 2020

Book design by Andrea MacLeod

ISBN 978-1-9991496-0-4 (paperback)
ISBN 978-1-9991496-1-1 (ebook)

Published by Writing Pixels Publishing

www.ethicalprofitbook.com

*Thank you, Jenny, for giving me the push
to finally put these ideas into words.*

*My dearest gratitude to Aleks, who supported me
in so many ways that got me across the finish line.*

Contents

Acknowledgments

I must, first and foremost, thank the B Corporation community for all their support and time, generously given to help me write this book. Your leadership is admirable and necessary, and I am honoured to share your stories with the world.

The greatest thanks goes to those I interviewed, and who kindly shared their experiences, business processes, and wisdom, in order to help inspire other businesses to create a more sustainable world together. Bruce Taylor, Tobias Mueller-Glodde, Bettina Hoar, Flip Brown, Rose Yee, Timothy Yee, Rob Thomas, Mike Gifford, Carly Stein, and all the folks in the B Corp community who took the time to share their knowledge. Thank you. Your selflessness is inspiring.

There are many others who have helped me in small ways, from challenging my thinking, like my long-time friend Kate Bullemor, to those who shared their eco-friendly tips in passing, like Carl Friesen.

I am especially grateful to Krista Downey for designing my cover, as well as David Drascic, John Schrag, Stephanie Belau, Amanda Wondergem, Andrew Cheng and many others who provided great feedback that led to a cover design that I love and am proud of. Thanks for humouring me!

Particular thanks needs to be given to Andrea MacLeod, who did such a fantastic job designing my layout and assisting in more behind-the-scenes logistics than I ever thought possible. Publishing this book without your support would have been impossible.

This book would never have been written without the magnificent coaching of Jenny McKaig, who gently, but firmly, nudged me to write this book, which I've been holding onto for over ten years now.

Thank you to my editor, Mary-Margaret Scrimger, for your excellent work and for turning a pile of garbage into a readable, comprehensible book.

Special thanks to Heather Gamble for her advice over the years and sharing her wisdom, providing me with answers to problems like a fairy godmother.

There are others who have contributed through sharing research, such as Yvonne Lin, Panos Panagiotakopoulos, and Michael Smith, which helped in building a book built on facts.

To my partner, Aleks, who spent many days and nights picking up the domestic slack so that I could write. She also did the sexy job of checking my math, which is a pretty critical job for a book about finance but something no one wants to do for fun.

As is with most of these things, there will be others I have forgotten to thank, for which I ask your forgiveness. In the five years I've spent writing this book, I have learnt so much from my peers, colleagues, friends and passersby that have helped shape this book. I am grateful to everyone who has encouraged me along the way.

The Urgency for Change

B ees. They are the perfect example. A species integral to the ecological health of the world that are on the brink of extinction because businesses prioritize making a profit. This is just one case of unethical decisions putting the environment at risk. In the U.S. alone, climate change disasters have already cost $1.7 trillion, according to NOAA. This number steadily increases every year we procrastinate in solving the climate crisis. According to a recent paper published in the *Proceedings of the National Academy of Sciences*, the cost of climate change increases exponentially. This doesn't include the cost to the rest of the world and I personally think it's a conservative and limited estimate. How do you put a dollar value on the extinction of an entire species? We don't even truly understand how the inter-dependencies of our ecology work, so to base the value of bees purely on the benefit to the agriculture industry underestimates the importance of bees to the rest of society.

There is little need to make the business case for running environmentally and socially responsible companies. The economic devastation that climate change will have on the global economy is undeniable. Consider the human, labour, and resource costs of climate change refugees. These are entire populations displaced because their homelands have been washed away in floods. Or engulfed in forest fires. Or destroyed by hurricanes or tornadoes. The ripple effects of drought, famine, floods, fire, and other natural disasters have had a far-reaching impact in many countries already. For some, it has led to civil wars, while others have gone bankrupt. The devastating destruction to those who pick up the pieces after a disaster is a huge cost to bear individually, as well as by society, if aid is offered.

These are some highlights of living in a society that has abandoned environmental and social responsibility. One of the biggest issues with conventional business models is the hidden costs that are not factored into a product or business but society pays for through other avenues. Either by declining health paired with rising health care costs, taxpayer-funded pollution clean-up, allocation of human and natural resources—the list goes on and on. These costs must be included in business planning moving forward if we intend to build a better future not just for our kids but for our species.

Even if following this guide seems like a lot, I invite you to look through it and find one thing you can *immediately implement* into your business. The journey of becoming more environmentally-friendly begins with a single action. If all entrepreneurs did one thing, we would collectively make an exponential impact. There are more entrepreneurs than ever and it's important to start with the right base, so that as you grow you can save money (yes, environmental choices can save you money) while feeding your soul, knowing you're making the best decision for your work and your world.

Small businesses and entrepreneurs make up 98%+ (BDC) of the economy and taxpayer dollars. Never forget how powerful you are. Everything you do, every change you make, has a ripple effect you cannot begin to imagine.

So let's embark on this journey to creating a better world with a new and sustainable economy.

SECTION I

WHY YOU SHOULD CARE

Everyone is in different stages of their sustainability journey, and I want to honour that and help you along the way. This section is for folks who are new to sustainability or want more background information into what sustainability actually means for your business.

Sustainability is multi-faceted, a term used to encompass the many aspects that are involved in making a business profitable long-term. Sustainability in business includes everything from strong sales to ensure your business is viable year-on-year to managing your people well so you have employees to keep the doors open. These next chapters are for those who wish to learn how to view their business finances from a more holistic perspective, and why it is important to do so.

If you already have some background knowledge on sustainable business practices, or have already seen the benefits of implementing sustainable business practices and want some more ideas for next steps you can take, feel free to skip to Sections II or III. Section II dives into more of the nitty-gritty on how to be sustainable and start saving money in a shorter time frame. These are recommendations that apply to a variety of industries and business stages, so you can take something away and run with it immediately.

Section III goes further with technical and financial recommendations, such as why you should move to a credit union and how to have a massive impact by moving your retirement funds into ethical investments. These recommendations are for those who are willing to push through the mental blocks we create around perceived financial difficulties, but have a tangible long-term benefit to moving to a sustainable economy.

One

The Current State of Affairs. How Did We Get Here?

Our society is built on capitalism that, as said previously, doesn't calculate the full cost of doing business. Industries are built entirely on hidden costs that are not factored into the final price of an item. For example, consider a cheap plastic item you can buy from a dollar store, like disposable forks or straws. What does that cost actually pay for?

If you consider how that plastic disposable item got to the store, and what will happen with it afterwards, that $1 to $2 has to cover a lot. Raw oil had to be extracted from a mine, shipped to a refinery, processed, shipped to a factory to be processed further into the plastic item, which is then packaged and shipped to the distribution centre before being shipped to the store where you bought it. Once you are done with it, a city garbage truck needs to drive to your house to collect it and then drive it to the recycling facility, if one exists in your area, or to the local landfill.

This product is one piece in a larger picture, but almost all of our material products are created in this way. But does it account for the destruction inflicted on the environment by the mine cutting down trees and digging up the earth to extract the oil? If there were any oil spills or accidents, have those costs been accounted for? What about the fuel to transport the raw materials between the mine and the refinery and then on to the distribution centre and retail stores? Then there is the energy used in the process of refining it, and the machine's energy to create the plastic and cut it into each disposable item. Not to mention the cost of disposing the item, paid for by taxpayers to the local government. There are also workers to consider in each step of this process, from the mines to the factories to the disposal, and the potential harm to their health due to being exposed to pollution over time, health care costs that are subsidized by taxpayers.

When each piece of a product's lifecycle is considered, from resource extraction to the landfill or recycling, everything we buy should cost a lot more than it does now, once everything is accounted for. Except a business doesn't have to pay the earth for cutting down a tree or a rain cloud for providing the water harvested. If it did, the Industrial Revolution may have developed quite differently.

Fossil fuels enabled this capitalistic economy to grow exponentially, but without truly incorporating the real environmental cost, including the impact on vulnerable communities. Western countries have amassed greater wealth than at any time in history; greatly improved human lives according to all metrics from life expectancy to health care access; invented many things to make our lives more convenient; created technology that allows us to buy almost anything online and have it delivered to our door. But at what cost? To paraphrase the state of affairs, Paul Hawken said, "Our economy by and large operates by stealing the future, selling it in the present, and calling it GDP."

Anti-environment companies are at a tough stage, barely in compliance with current environmental statutes or complaining vehemently about the cost compliance laws have on their business. It's an unfortunate attitude because these laws exist for a reason. History shows us that, time and time again, unless there are regulations requiring businesses to act in accordance with the greater good, human greed will override common sense. For example, business greed is the reason we need anti-corruption and insider trading laws, because at one point someone abused the power of their position to subvert the system and get rich at the expense of others. This is also the case for things like health and safety, labour laws, environmental protection, consumer protection, taxation, etc.

The above-mentioned businesses are modelled on the past and are not building to serve the future. They are operating businesses that can barely keep up with the present. Those who are ready to do what is necessary right now—build a business in tandem with society and our environment—are at the base necessity of business. In order to future-proof one's business, avoiding going the way of BlockBuster Video, we have to build environmental costs into our business *while remaining profitable.*

William McDonough and Michael Braungart accurately summed up our production outlook in their book, *Cradle to Cradle.*

Society has designed business production that:

- Puts billions of toxic material into the air, water, and soil every year
- Produces some materials so dangerous they will require constant vigilance by future generations
- Results in gigantic amounts of waste
- Puts valuable materials in holes all over the planet where they can never be retrieved
- Requires thousands of complex regulations, not to keep people and natural systems safe, but rather to keep them from being poisoned too quickly
- Measures productivity by how few people it takes to accomplish a task, essentially efficiency
- Creates prosperity by digging up or cutting down natural resources and then burying or burning them
- Erodes the diversity of species and cultural practices

Of course, the industrialists, engineers, inventors, and other minds behind the Industrial Revolution never intended such consequences. In fact, the Industrial Revolution as a whole wasn't designed. It took shape gradually, as problems were identified and solutions were implemented to take advantage of opportunities in an unprecedented period of massive and rapid change (McDonough & Braungart, pg. 18).

So, how did we get here?

A major contributor to the advancement of business and industry during the Industrial Revolution was coal. It replaced wood as an energy source, which enabled machines to produce more goods at a cheaper cost. This helped accelerate economic growth and continued in a positive feedback loop that saw advances and inventions towards our current global economy. Up until that point, there had not been such explosive population and economic growth. As businesses grew, however, the need for regulation also increased, resulting in unions who advocated for weekends, sick leave, vacations, and many of our current labour laws that are taken for granted.

Over time, governments began to introduce laws and taxes to either encourage or discourage certain business activities. Business laws were created to protect company founders as the ones taking a risk on a new venture. In North America in particular, business laws encouraged entrepreneurship and the investment in such businesses. The invention of the stock market allowed for other owners to make a profit from investing in a business without direct management or involvement, and eventually forcing managers to focus on maximizing that profit. However, this has also resulted in a lack of regulation protecting other business stakeholders, such as suppliers, consumers, governments, the public, and the environment. Because the Industrial Revolution was entirely new in the history of humankind, we've been making it up as we go along ever since. But along the way scientists and business leaders alike have been calling for businesses to be accountable to more than just profit. None of this would have been possible without using coal and oil to jump start the Industrial Revolution, but at the time the environmental cost was not accounted for in any way.

There is no denying it. The climate crisis exists because industries focused their business decision-making on only one factor: profit. And the other costs have been devastating. Concerns over the impact of businesses on the environment reach as far back as the 1930s, but the sustainability movement that we know today was set into motion in the 1950s with Rachel Carson's ground-breaking book, *Silent Spring*. She presented shocking evidence that spraying poisons was bad for one's health, killed nearby plants and animals, and damaged the environment by poisoning waterways and seeping into our food. This ignited what would become the tree hugging hippie movement of ordinary people wanting to protect the environment, and they were considered the enemy of conventional business. They were the ones who were public about pushing businesses to change their practices. However, businesses only began adopting environmentally-friendly business models en masse over the past thirty years.

Yet still, we have many products with labels like this one, highlighted in William McDonough's TED Talk "Cradle to Cradle Design":

This is a rubber duck. It comes in California with a warning: "This product contains chemicals known by the State of California to cause cancer and birth defects or other reproductive harm." This is a bird. What kind of culture would produce a product of this kind and then label it and sell it to children? I think we have a design problem.

How can we continue operating our businesses in this manner when we know that it is robbing us of our health, environmental sustainability, economic stability, and future? We can no longer wait for regulations to force us to consider the future of the role of business in society. Businesses must take a leading role in the sustainability movement. There is no magic bullet solution for climate change—everyone, everywhere must do what they can to contribute to reducing the impact of climate change if we want to have a chance at protecting our future. Rather than continue waiting for research, science, and technology to advance to the point necessary, we can take power into our own hands. We have a golden opportunity at this time, as sustainable business has never been more relevant or profitable.

It's just good business.

Two

The First Step: Myth Busting

I hope to refute pervasive myths that prevent small businesses and entrepreneurs from focusing on sustainable business endeavours. If more time was devoted to implementing sustainable business practices than complaining about these myths, we would be further ahead on improving our sustainable solutions.

MYTH: IT WILL COST YOUR COMPANY MORE

There are several books and case studies showcasing the exact opposite, that environmentally responsible business actually outperforms the business-as-usual mentality. Bob Willard, author of *The Sustainable Advantage*, has studied environmentally-friendly business practices and found a 40% increase in profits for those that strengthen their commitments to environmentally and socially responsible business policies. This is compared to similar companies running their business without sustainability practices.

That's a huge advantage. Can you imagine having 40% more profit? If this is the case with large companies, imagine the gains in your small business. If you could increase profits by 40% tomorrow, how willing would you be to learn how to do it?

It's possible for any business to implement changes that are both sustainable and increase profit, even in the short-term. This is why implementing a strategic plan to first find low-hanging fruit is optimal. By examining your business and listening to the feedback of your employees, mentors, and colleagues, you can make quick-and-easy changes that fund longer-term sustainable investments. For example, eliminating paper consumption can save a business hundreds of dollars. These savings can be used to purchase LED lights that will save on energy costs. These electricity savings can be used to buy a waste-free coffee maker or a subscription to TerraCycle. The savings from garbage disposal can be used to fund an energy audit, or to buy plants for your office to improve indoor air quality and reduce stress levels. These boosted productivity levels improve your profit, and continue to feed a positive feedback loop.

MYTH: THE GREEN ECONOMY IS A FAD

Environmental activism has been happening since the 1970s and is still around today, which is more than we can say for bell-bottom jeans. It continues to gain traction with each subsequent generation coming into the workforce, who are concerned with their future. As they obtain more disposable income, millennials are interested in spending it on products in the sustainable economy. This can be seen in the various products and industries that millennials are said to be killing. Golf is one such industry, with its premium price coupled with the use of large swaths of land that could instead be a forest or parkland. Golf courses are having increasing trouble sustaining their business.

Meanwhile, the sustainable product market has been booming. It has been growing year over year and by 2018 was worth over $128 billion in the U.S. alone, according to Nielsen. Nielsen also reported that 90% of millennials, aged 21 to 34, are willing to pay more for products that contain sustainable ingredients.

This is capitalism at work, where consumers are voting with their dollars for sustainable products. Even when the competitor is cheaper, but importantly, made unsustainably, millennials overwhelmingly chose the sustainable option. The market for sustainable products is increasing, cannibalizing the market share of those products that are not made sustainably. If you have a product-based business and are not investing in sustainability, the long-term success of your business is in jeopardy.

MYTH: GREEN PRODUCTS ARE JUST A MARKETING PLOY

This myth is entwined with larger companies presenting themselves as eco-friendly only to be exposed as frauds, pretending to care about the planet. The deception of using products that are harmful to the environment, or manufactured in overseas plants with safety and human rights violations, is deplorable.

However, it is unfair to write-off all products and companies making sustainability claims. There are, for example, companies like Hero Certified Burger who are committed to sustainability throughout their supply chain, but do not use it as the crux of their marketing. Other companies, like Unilever, are very public about their commitment to sustainability. In September 2019, they announced all their sites across the world were powered by renewable grid energy, furthering their commitment to sustainability in all facets of their business.

This trend shows no sign of slowing down, as more multinational and billion-dollar companies announce or illustrate their plans to reduce their environmental impact.

MYTH: ECO-FRIENDLY EQUATES TO MEDIOCRE PRODUCTS

Words of caution here: There is a misconception in North America's mass market that eco-friendly equates to mediocre products. This myth originates from the last century, when the environmentally conscious consumer had little choice, and the items available at the time were not as effective as the mainstream alternatives. Eco-friendly products have come a long way in the last two decades. They tend to do the same job, last longer, and do not destroy fragile ecosystems in the process. As mentioned above, market share growth has encouraged competition, which is driving quality improvements in this sector. Cleaning products, for example, may be slightly less effective or fast-acting, but create a healthier space and decrease costs on things like health care. This is especially important in buildings with poor air quality or circulation. If your office is regularly cleaned, you do not need a harsh, environmentally-toxic cleaner to combat stains or ingrained dirt.

MYTH: THERE IS ONLY ONE WAY TO DO SUSTAINABILITY

Here's an important fact about sustainability: it's complicated. One size does not fit all, and not all solutions are applicable or relevant to your situation. This is why it is important to be constantly learning and do what you can. Never dismiss what your business **can** do, no matter how small.

Depending on where you live, you may have more or less access to renewable energy, or recycling and composting facilities, which means to be more sustainable may include advocating for these things in your area, beyond adopting these practices.

Sustainability for a manufacturer of goods looks completely different than a professional service provider or a travel company. Sustainability will look different again for a farmer, or airline, or internet-based company. At the same time, one business can learn a lot from what another business does, even if it is in another industry.

MYTH: SUSTAINABILITY IS NOT PROFITABLE

You may think I'm biased, given I'm writing an entire book about why sustainability is profitable, but research, case studies, and financial data all show sustainability to be profitable. Short-term thinking or unethical or environment disregard eventually catches up to a business. A large portion of expenses related to unethical business behaviour are related to fines or legal fees, but also employee attrition, waste, insurance premiums, regulatory compliance, etc. These are all business expenses that can be reduced when including sustainability business practices.

In 2011, the sportswear company Puma ran a case study of their 2010 finances, accounting for their carbon footprint and environmental impact to see what it would do to their profitability. They found their €202 million profit disappeared. This was a wake-up call to look at what sustainable practices they could implement in all areas of business to reduce waste and improve their profitability long-term.

There have also been studies done to evaluate the potential cost of climate change. Estimates vary on this, but one thing is certain: increased damage to infrastructure via storms, flooding, fires, etc., will cost us individually and collectively through taxpayer-funded repairs.

Alternatively, there are companies who have become very profitable through incorporating sustainability into the core of their company. Unilever, Chipotle Mexican Grill, and Whole Foods are examples of billion-dollar companies founded on sustainable principles. I encourage you to keep reading this book if you need further proof of what sustainable profit looks like for you.

MYTH: I'M JUST ONE PERSON, MY IMPACT DOESN'T MATTER

Every action we take feeds our collective, social choices, which have far-reaching impacts that we may not know about or can't understand due to the chain of events that it takes to have products grown, mined, refined, molded, and shipped all around the world. Our personal sustainability journey is something we can take control of, and are able to do something to not just ease our own conscience, but also to help others in our community who wish to do the same but don't know how. Thinking our actions don't matter in the grand scheme of things completely erases our existence in society, as if our buying habits, our business habits, don't influence the business choices of others. This is a normal feeling but it's simply not true. We do not do anything in isolation.

Nicole Pasulka illustrates this in her article, *Running the Numbers*:

The problem is this cumulative effect from the behaviors of hundreds of millions of individuals. Each person looks around at their own behavior, and it doesn't look all that bad. What we each have to expand our consciousness to hold is that the cumulative effect of hundreds of millions of individual consumer decisions is causing the worldwide destruction of our environment... The only way we have of relating to these incredibly important facts about our mass consumption is statistics. And the problem with stats is they're so dry and emotionless. If we're going to be motivated as a culture to change our behavior, then we're going to have to find a deep motivation.

Because taking care of our environment is everyone's responsibility, no one takes personal responsibility in the same way that the bystander effect results in inaction during an emergency. We as consumers and business owners need to recognize that our contributions matter, and that every action adds up, regardless of the scope of those actions.

Cumulative impact is important to remember in anything that impacts our society. For example, we pay taxes to collectively pay for education, the roads we drive on, etc. As an individual, you may only pay $5,000 to $10,000 in taxes in a given year. If you tried to build a road or fund a school, your $10,000 in taxes wouldn't get you very far. However, when everyone in the country pools that money together, as well as the taxes from businesses, you can build roads that not only get you to work, but can get you to the other side of the country.

There is a mindset shift here that I would like you to consider. Rather than thinking your impact doesn't matter, consider approaching it as, "I am doing everything I can to protect the future of my business and the planet for future generations." You may not be able to have a completely positive impact right now, but as mentioned at the start of this book, it is important to make continual changes and improve as you can.

MYTH: SUSTAINABILITY IS TOO HARD TO IMPLEMENT IN MY BUSINESS

I will admit that if you were to implement every possible sustainable action into your business practices, it would be hard, especially if you are not familiar with what that means. Designing a business with processes that defy norms and established practices to disrupt an industry is hard.

Change is hard!

But change is important. It's inevitable. It's become par for the course in the business world, especially with the influx of technology, which is accelerating and amplifying a changing business landscape around the world. Innovation and disruption are what led to the bankruptcy of Blockbuster and the rise of Netflix. It did not happen overnight, remember, but it was to the detriment of Blockbuster that they did not see Netflix as viable competition until it was too late. The time is now for any company dismissing sustainability as a fad to realize if they do not change their businesses now, they may not be around in the future.

Rather than considering implementing sustainable business practices as hard or future-proofing, consider them as *opportunities*. Every day the sustainable economy creates more jobs, adds more value to the economy, and more employees are interested in working for a company that protects the environment and the future. Millennial consumers demand this change, and they are the generation of consumers and workers who are fueling this economic trend more than ever.

One company who has embraced this is Patagonia. They see sustainability to be their competitive edge. They've worked extensively on all aspects of their business to create sustainable conditions in their supply chain, from living wages to recycling materials, to being 100% powered by renewable energy in the U.S. Their mission is to create the best product while causing no harm to the environment and to encourage their customers to connect with nature, which has known mental health and stress-reduction benefits. They've made extremely loyal customers for their uncompromising quality, great customer service, and dedication to making their employees happy. All these facets have been self-confessed by CEO Rose Marcario to be hard, and this is why they do them: Patagonia has a long history of expecting business to evolve to serve humanity, and they are exemplifying this through their actions.

MYTH: IT'S TOO TIME CONSUMING

This myth ties into the myth, discussed later, that only big companies can incorporate sustainability into their business practices. The idea that it's too time-consuming may stem from the idea that you need to change everything immediately, which doesn't work for everyone. It doesn't take a lot of time to decide to incorporate sustainability into your business—by the end of this book you should have some ideas of things you can readily implement. Then all it takes is a commitment to follow through.

Additionally, things like switching your business suppliers to ones that use less packaging, source their products sustainability, or pay a living wage does not take much time or effort to implement. If you want an example of some companies already doing this, see 'Appendix B: Resources' at the back of this book.

To say sustainability is too time-consuming is very much an excuse—it's not like having to implement new inventory or customer relationship management (CRM) software. Sustainable business practices will be critical to the future of making it as a business. Getting ahead of the curve will save time and money in the long-term and, ultimately, be easier when you can implement them on your own timeline instead of a regulated one.

MYTH: NO ONE ELSE IS DOING IT

It surprises me that this is still a myth, because it seems like no matter where you look—on TV, Youtube, Instagram, Reddit, Twitter, Facebook—people are constantly sharing tips for lifestyle sustainability or reusing and recycling. These posts or videos are constantly shared and more are uploaded, so, statistically, many people must be doing sustainability. It gets views, likes, shares, eyeballs, and advertising dollars, which are all important measures of success in today's online work. And it's why this content continues to be made.

A skeptic may say this isn't content made for business, but I would contest that many of these ideas can be applied to the business world with a little adjustment and creativity.

I remember fifteen or so years ago, watching a *60 Minutes* report in Australia about a woman who had bought an electric car back when almost no one was doing sustainability and had installed solar panels on her roof, so only had a $2 monthly electricity bill. In a country that has the highest electricity costs in the Western world, this was shocking. And incredibly eye-opening.

I realized then that while we were busy making excuses, others were implementing sustainable business practices and saving a lot of money, without fanfare, or waiting for it to be trendy, or even waiting to have all the information available to them. They just made the choice that was best for the environment, and it saved them thousands of dollars in electricity and fuel each year.

MYTH: WHO CARES?

As mentioned above, statistically many, many people already care about sustainability. Millennials especially consider sustainability to be an important consideration when buying from a company and are willing to pay more for sustainable goods. There have been multiple reports and studies on climate change, including by the UN, that concluded that climate change is the greatest challenge facing the younger generations. More and more, we're learning how our actions impact and harm others, even those on the other side of the world. We can no longer afford, both financially and morally, to not care.

Your consumers care more about sustainability, and if your target audience, or future target audience, cares about sustainability, your company will too in order to remain competitive in the future.

Financially, there are many reasons to care about sustainability. Aside from Bob Willard's findings that businesses who implement sustainable practices are 40% more profitable than their competitors, your insurance company cares a lot about climate change. As an industry, their profits are hugely impacted by climate-related disasters. They've already run the numbers and done the risk analysis on sustainability, and offer lower premiums to multinational and manufacturing companies adopting sustainable practices. This is also why your policy covers less and less these days.

MYTH: SUSTAINABILITY REQUIRES A LOT OF STAFF TIME

Many companies, including large ones, devote less time and staff to sustainable initiatives than you might expect. Most sustainability teams are a few people at most, but their effect is felt company-wide because there is a top-down attitude prioritizing sustainability and the sustainability team's efforts. This makes their work effective and makes sure their plans or ideas are implemented and fairly evaluated. Staff throughout the company are aware that sustainability is important and that improvements are always welcome.

Your business might not have a lot of staff yet, and the idea of creating a whole team might seem like a lot of investment for your business. In that case, ask your staff who would be willing to take on the sustainability advocate role in your company. Chances are, at least one person at your company cares about this, given 70% of millennials want to work somewhere with a strong environmental agenda. The important thing is to give them enough time and resources to work on this. If your employees are already overworked, prioritizing any business development will be difficult. The selected employees also need the authority to make changes and introduce their systems, processes, ideas, and innovations to make your company more sustainable. I promise they have good ideas. All you have to do is listen to them.

MYTH: GOVERNMENT INTERVENTION IS NOT NECESSARY

As I will explain in further detail in this chapter with a story about Enron, legal and government regulation are very important to assure some businesses do not just the legal thing, but the ethical thing.

In the past, we've seen multinationals moving their companies to countries that don't have the same legal and governmental oversights, to save money and take advantage of the local resources. Regularly, fines are issued to North American businesses that break the law, intentionally or not. In an age when any competitive edge is seen as paramount to increasing profits and market share, more than once a business has cut corners or engaged in unethical behaviour to gain that competitive edge.

Business has always attempted to use loopholes to avoid fiduciary responsibility. Given that statistically there are more CEOs who are psychopaths, this behaviour should not be surprising. This is why it is important for the government to step in and regulate businesses—to ensure they are abiding by human rights codes, fair wage laws, environmental protections, etc.

When the largest polluters refuse to act in the best interest of people and the planet, it is necessary for the governments of the world to intervene. To date, business has been slow to adopt sustainability practices. We are now at a time-critical need for government to impose clear regulations protecting people and planet.

MYTH: SUSTAINABILITY FOCUSES ONLY ON THE ENVIRONMENT

As we established in the Section I introduction, sustainability is a multi-faceted, holistic approach to sustaining a good future for businesses, people, and the planet. It incorporates a cradle-to-cradle approach as much as possible. (If you haven't watched William McDonald's TED Talk yet, I highly encourage you to do so.) The environment is a big component of sustainability, as it is currently the one least accounted for in traditional business language. However, sustainability is also concerned with fostering healthy communities, supporting workers through paying a living wage, and encouraging career development and continual education. Keeping your employees happy is also very sustainable, as you retain company knowledge, and employee turnover is very expensive. Sure, you can run a company with unhappy employees and high turnover, but it is not likely to be as profitable, and you'll never reach peak efficiency and productivity.

Paying taxes and maintaining good asset management is also a facet of sustainability, as society needs taxes to function and we need to pay for health care, roads, and whatnot. Managing assets ensures they last longer, require fewer resources overall, and are replaced less often. All these contribute to a more sustainable business.

MYTH: CORPORATE SOCIAL RESPONSIBILITY (CSR) IS ONLY FOR LARGE COMPANIES

Large companies have seemingly endless resources to dedicate to environmental and social improvements. You know, as a creative and dexterous entrepreneur, that you can't approach problems the same way as a large business. You have to approach the challenge differently, through innovating and adapting. But just like large companies can see a huge benefit from investing in greening their company, there are significant gains to be made in smaller companies as well.

There are countless examples of good things coming from companies willingly investing in corporate social responsibility—and many failures that arise from those that do not. Throughout this book, we will explore a few case studies you may or may not know about to learn facets of success and failure from ethical companies and unethical practices.

I want to share an important story that illustrates the cost of multiple 'business as usual' practices and mindsets—and what happens to those who stretch the rules.

Enron: Business Monstrosity? Excellent Case Study? Both?

Enron is now a synonym for fraud and corruption. It was a company that caused changes in business and accounting laws because it deceived its employees, shareholders, and customers until the truth caught up with them. Fake accounts, falsified documents, exploitation of accounting loopholes, executives stealing, insider trading—this was a legal and accounting drama that shook the world.

Before the scandal, Enron was hailed by *Fortune* magazine, won multiple prestigious business awards, and their stock price grew steadily. Their accountants, Arthur Andersen LLP, enabled the fraud and even advised them on the how. The collapse of Enron caused economic devastation for many people, including employees, shareholders, and associates.

At the height of Enron's business, Arthur Andersen LLP was the fifth largest accounting firm *in the world*. It reported $9.3 million in revenue in 2001 prior to the scandal and, reasonably, was considered a successful business. And while most of the consultants and people who worked for Arthur Andersen LLP would have had strong ethics and would have been considered bright, capable, employable consultants, their reputation was tarnished following the collapse of Enron. Arthur Andersen LLP soon had the same fate. The association with Enron, including the terrible publicity and public fallout, led to clients leaving Arthur Andersen LLP in droves. Within a year, their business was in shambles and, not long after, they dissolved the company. Unethical business practices that focused solely on bottom line profit, to the exclusion of all else, proved to be a terrible business decision. Had Arthur Anderson LLP acted in accordance with the interests of their stakeholders, such as customers and the public, they would have exposed the fraud much sooner, saved the U.S. economy millions of dollars, and likely won the loyalty of their clients and trust of the public. Had they chosen differently, Arthur Andersen LLP had the potential to become the #1 accounting firm in the world. Would you not want to work with the company that prevented an economic catastrophe? Instead, their misconduct forced lawmakers to introduce regulation to protect stakeholders, and the accounting profession to elevate its own standards of practice. This meant additional requirements for an industry where most people were doing the right thing—now, everyone has to deal with more red tape because of a few bad apples.

Enron is an important example of why regulation is important to ensure larger companies comply with good governance and ethical practices. Unfortunately, there will always be a few people who exploit others or do business unethically, and without regulation it is difficult to get justice or to stop those practices. It's also why it's important to include ethical practices in your business. Given the recent push for increased environmental regulation and fiduciary duties to increase governance, embedding these practices into every part of your business will help ensure your success in the future.

So let's do this.

Three

What is Sustainability?

O ne of the greatest challenges of the sustainability movement has been committing to a name. You've probably heard of various ways to describe sustainability over the years: eco-friendly, green business, environmentally-friendly, socially responsible, corporate social responsibility, triple-bottom-line accounting, realistic accounting, asset management, renewable energy, green buildings, circular economy, cradle-to-cradle, zero-waste—the list goes on.

The inconsistent naming even on what to call climate change has caused confusion over time. Confusion has enabled inaction, which is the opposite of what the movement is going for. I encountered all of the above names in researching this book, and while to me it all means the same thing, for some this has not been the case.

So throughout this book, we are going to use the term 'sustainability' as an all-encompassing term. Sustainability covers many facets of what is necessary to have a sustainable business, economy, and future. The term was defined by the United Nations in 1987 as:

Sustainable development is development that meets the needs of the present without compromising the ability of future generations to meet their own needs. It contains within it two key concepts: the concept of 'needs', in particular the essential needs of the world's poor, to which overriding priority should be given; and the idea of limitations imposed by the state of technology and social organization on the environment's ability to meet present and future needs. (Our Common Future, 1987)

In essence, sustainability is focused on meeting the needs of today's world without compromising our children's capacity to meet their own needs. The UN also gives priority to the world's poor, as it is critical that their development not be impeded. For many decades now, we have been consuming more resources than our planet provides, so we have been stealing the future's capacity to satisfy their needs.

To me, sustainability encompasses everything from protecting and expanding carbon sinks; fragile ecosystems; wildlife; rivers; our oceans; paying one's fair share of taxes; becoming a zero-waste society; triple-bottom-line accounting; reducing carbon emissions; preventing oil spills and other hazardous waste leaks; valuing our natural resources and protecting them legally; implementing a carbon tax; and so much more.

One critical element of sustainability is reducing waste. William McDonough's cradle-to-cradle approach is that there is no waste when throwing something away. Everything goes somewhere and waste products can become another's food. Your waste is a dung beetle's feast. What we consider waste can actually be reused or recycled. Compost is used as fertilizer, old clothes and items can be donated to thrift stores, having a bottle-return policy for your customers—the list goes on. The Body Shop, an international franchise famous for their ethical standards, implemented a refillable bottle policy for customers who brought back the containers to the first store, back in 1970 when the first store opened. This was not primarily to reduce waste, although it was a great by-product. The owner did this because she didn't have enough money to buy more containers when her original supply ran out. This need to be frugal helped pioneer many of The Body Shop's environmental practices, ultimately reducing the waste their company produced while saving them money, which was critical in their early days of growth.

The Body Shop was built on disrupting its industry, and structured its business in a way that sourced raw materials in an unconventional, ethical, and organic way. It also was very outspoken about animal testing, which was the standard at the time. Their environmental efforts were a natural extension of rewriting the rules of business, which is very common today.

Also, an important note here, waste doesn't just disappear because we no longer see it. Ensuring that material doesn't go to landfills, which is not conducive to decomposition, is the objective. Keeping an object as is, being used to its fullest capacity, is the objective. So, ensuring that your car is running and in tip top condition, using your reusable coffee mug every morning for as long as possible, and ensuring energy isn't being used unnecessarily in your business are all part of decreasing your waste.

Recycling, while it is not the solution, is a tool for decreasing waste. When a plastic bottle no longer has a use, it is recycled. It can have a second life as a park bench, decks, playground equipment or even become another plastic bottle. However, this takes energy, so using an object for as long as possible is the best solution to decreasing waste. Back to *Cradle to Cradle*:

> *Waste is a product that companies create through spending resources and money, yet adds no value to the business. Then business[es] often have to spend money to dispose or treat this waste. Waste is a huge cost to business in North America. The ratio for the U.S. economy as a whole is 6 percent product and 94 percent non-product.*

This means almost 95% of the money you are spending in your business is not to create the product, but on everything else. Gil Friend's *The Truth About Green Business* further breaks down potential solutions to handling our waste addiction in the following ways:

1. **Reduce waste:** Process efficiency is imperative. Unfortunately, business competition and trade secrets have made us rather wasteful of Earth's resources. Instead of collaborating to share excess resources with other companies, each business has to buy or create their own stuff when it would be much more efficient and sustainable to share. There are many other things that your business can also look at such as pollution prevention, waste minimization, business process reengineering, and creating designs with the environment in

mind through redesign and re-specification of products, processes, and equipment.

2. **Waste as an asset:** The saying that one person's trash is another's treasure applies in business too. Consider this both internally and externally. Turning the waste of one process into the inputs of another can increase net yields. Internally, this can look like cycling scraps back into the product stream (wood pulp turned into recycled paper) or using waste heat from electrical generation to heat water. Externally, start with recycling and compost efforts and grow from there, depending on your business needs.

3. **Compostable waste:** Design your waste to be more digestible by the food chain or useful to an up or downstream vendor in your supply chain, and it becomes a product. At the very least, design your waste to be safely compostable so that if it ends up in a landfill or in a waterway, it will biodegrade and not harm the environment.

4. **Break the addiction to stuff:** Produce more value with fewer physical resources. This includes finding ways to get more done with less, or ways to allow customers to buy more services from you and less product. Ask questions like, "Will buying this help make us more efficient?" and "Once I've used this product until the end of its useful life, how easy is it to recycle or find a new use for it?" so that your business isn't buying things for the sake of it and wasting money in the process.

5. **Measure what matters:** Use key performance indicators to measure your progress toward your holistic business goals. This could be internally designed measures or through something like B Corporation, if you're at a loss for where to start (more on this later).

The tremendous amount of energy and resources it takes to make stuff—even sustainable, environmentally-responsible stuff—is not reflected in our rapid consumption and discarding of our material goods. Fashion is an industry that exemplifies this. There is fast fashion, where there are new clothes on the racks every three to four months that are cheap and low quality, designed to wear out and be replaced quickly. There are designer brands that are well made and very expensive, though are not necessarily more ethical in their business decisions, due to sweatshops and poor sustainability practices. Then there is ethical fashion, brands created because the founders were concerned with the unsustainable environmental and unsafe working practices common in the fashion industry. Their products are designed to be higher quality and longer lasting, while paying a living wage to those who make the clothing and sourcing fabrics that are sustainably grown and harvested. Nonetheless, all of these clothes end up in landfills unless your mall is lucky enough to have a clothes recycling drop off.

This is why the Environmental Protection Agency says we generate an average of 250 million tons of trash per year, roughly 814 pounds per person. This is only personal waste and doesn't include the waste produced by small business and industrial waste. As businesses, we contribute to 70-75% of the waste chain. Diverting waste, reducing our consumption, and reusing instead of buying new are easy ways to better manage the waste our society produces.

The best part is, when you are able to minimize your waste, you save money!

A great example of this is a condominium building in Toronto, Ontario, that is considered one of the greenest condos in Toronto. There are over 1,000 residents in this building of 286 units, and they only throw out one bin of garbage every month. They did this by ensuring each resident recycled everything correctly, with the maintenance staff collecting recycling directly from each door. If the recycling was not correct, it would not be collected and the superintendent would educate the residents on the correct recycling to include. They implemented a compost program, which was also collected directly from residents and education was provided on what to include.

Once this was in place, they no longer had multiple garbage bins in their garbage room, so they converted a section into an exchange station. Residents who no longer wanted an item that was in otherwise good condition could put it in this room and other residents could take it if they had a use for it. This dramatic decrease in their landfill waste led to a $100 savings per month for every resident in the building. The building also implemented water and energy savings plans, further reducing their condo maintenance fees.

These few initiatives alone have diverted tonnes of waste from the landfill and saved thousands of dollars each year. How they got to this point isn't particularly revolutionary or transformative, they just had a superintendent who had the will and patience to help implement their sustainable initiatives. Similar savings and waste diversion is possible in your building and your business—as long as there is a commitment to them and support provided to help them succeed.

At this time, having a sustainable business is non-negotiable. As Jonathon Porritt rightfully says in his book, *Capitalism as if the World Matters*, "the opposite of sustainability is extinction." He is referring to both the extinction of your business by going bankrupt and the extinction of our way of life.

Averting a climate crisis is a huge undertaking and will not be solved with a magic bullet solution. Science and technology alone cannot do what is necessary in the time we have left. To avert the climate crisis, everyone on Earth must do whatever they can to become more sustainable. There is no way to limit climate change otherwise. We have used excuses for decades to justify our inaction, yet forget that collectively, small businesses wield more than half the economic power in North America. This number is higher for other countries. Changing business practices to be more sustainable is one critical part of the solution to climate change.

Four

The Case for Making Your Business Sustainable

E arlier I mentioned B Corporation, which is a certification process for any business to have an external validation that they are doing good in the world. Think of it like Fair Trade is for coffee, B Corporation is for business. It was born in the U.S. due to their business laws making it illegal for a business to focus on anything but bottom line profit, even if that would ultimately hurt the business in the long-term. The U.S. Corporations Act has justified business focus on profit to the exclusion of all else, but becoming a B Corporation (or B Corp) allows businesses to prioritise other factors that make a business both sustainable and profitable, in particular, once a business grows in size where there are many outside factors that affect day-to-day operations.

B Corporation is a growing movement across the world, with tens of thousands of businesses using their certification process as a way to help measure their progress on a year-by-year basis to see how they perform compared to other small businesses and even businesses in similar industries. The B Corp assessment tool is incredibly useful for a small business to utilise to manage and measure sustainability initiatives.

Given that the biggest challenge in making your business sustainable is that half the time you don't even know where to start, the B Corp assessment can help show you what is possible and most pressing for your business. You can also choose to focus on areas that are important to your business, such as the environment or your community engagement.

Otherwise, the upfront costs and multiple behavioural changes of becoming sustainable can seem daunting and turn people away. For example, organic food is considered more expensive, albeit sometimes only marginally, than non-organic food. For price-conscious consumers, a few cents can make the difference of what to buy. In recent years, companies have developed sustainable products at price points that are competitive and with quality that is as good as or better than conventional products. This is part of why there has been more traction in recent years for sustainable products. But in the end, sustainable products are less expensive because of the reduced impact on the planet, as they are accounting for the full lifetime of that product, from raw material to, hopefully, recycling it into the next product.

Being financially savvy is not always part of the entrepreneur skill set, so it can be difficult to calculate the difference in financial expenditure between the high upfront costs of buying a hybrid car versus an SUV that is cheaper upfront but has higher maintenance in the long-term. Sure, you may like an SUV and the image it creates, but is it really worth an extra $1,000 a year out of your pocket? Especially when your business has so many other expenses, choosing the best option for the long-term can impact your success. Buying a new or used vehicle is a similar consideration. Are the savings on the used car worth the additional maintenance costs?

All companies should have hybrid company cars if they need to own a car. Let's break down the savings to show why it makes business sense:

- **Microcars:** Best for companies that operate out of urban centres, have minimal long distance travel, and have a small staff of contractors or employees.
- **Hybrid car:** Most economic and practical. It includes mileage, financial options similar to a typical company car, and allows for long distance trips in a business as usual fashion until electric cars are more common and practical.
- **Conventional car:** Long-term costs are higher with rising gasoline costs including pollution that increase personal taxes for clean-up, although it isn't listed as an expense on the company books (at least not yet).

- **Ride shares:** Zipcar, Car2Go, and Enterprise, to name a few, allow you to rent a car by the hour. Some, like Car2Go, allow you to take the short trip in one direction, whereas Zipcars and Enterprise must be returned to the same location. They are perfect for any occasion that you need a car for a minimal amount of time. They're increasingly becoming a replacement for company cars, as they are usually a much cheaper option than owning a car.

The car industry is a constantly changing landscape as new models with varying efficiency come out each year and more car manufacturers release hybrid or electric vehicles. When looking to buy or lease a new vehicle, consider comparing the options available by taking into account environmental factors in addition to the traditional considerations like:

- Government rebates available for hybrid or electric vehicles
- The rising costs of fuel making conventional vehicles more costly to operate
- The potential for a carbon tax on vehicles with emissions
- The maintenance costs over the life of the vehicle

These factors will change year over year and the type of vehicle that is best will be dependent on your usage. Conventional sedans can emit upwards of three tonnes of CO_2 into the atmosphere in a single year, so remember to consider that in your carbon footprint calculations.

This is just one example, and there are many more.

Often, the short-sightedness of the business world is the greatest downfall to lasting and significant change. Environmental changes may not cause cash to immediately flow in, and it can be hard for businesses to invest in large expenditures for the greater good. But these changes can help stop cash from flowing out. To be environmentally conscious is to implement a long-term vision that could create short-term cash problems or slower initial growth, which is at odds with how business is expected to work these days, but is better in the long run.

This could be said for our personal actions as well. Unfortunately, business often continues in an inefficient, environmentally destructive way simply because it has always been done that way. New environmental initiatives are incorrectly perceived as costly or inconvenient, and because the problem—such as dwindling fossil fuel supplies or excessive carbon in the atmosphere—isn't immediately obvious, these initiatives don't get the attention they deserve. Repressing one's ethics or morals, or not questioning them at all, seems easier and that contributes to the problem.

Does change seem too inconvenient? Well, *doing nothing* has far greater negative ramifications than the immediate pain and inconvenience of transition. Obscurity, falling from grace, and bankruptcy can become the fate of rigid businesses. This is the new age, where business is driven by consumer demand. The labour market, pushed by millennials, demands more meaningful and social consciousness from businesses. Companies that proritize corporate social responsibility or sustainability, and walk the walk by infusing B Corporation values into their business, are more likely to attract and retain the new worker.

Change can include supporting employees beyond the bare expectations. This includes paying a living wage (adjusting pay grades to reflect the cost of living in cities around the world), offering the same benefits to employees as are offered to management, subsidizing personal development and further education, encouraging social engagement through paid volunteer days, and implementing a health and wellness program for all employees. This is in addition to focusing on environmentally-conscious decision making.

Questions to ask when making an environmentally beneficial investment for your business, especially one that may seem costly in the short-term:

- **Question One:** Why is it important to buy this? Is it a future monetary savings or solely for ethical, moral, or personal reasons? Is it both?
- **Question Two:** Am I hesitating at the price because I don't have the money right now and the initial outlay is unfeasible at this moment?
- **Question Three:** What is the cost of not doing this? What are the immediate costs and what are the future costs? How much will it cost to continue doing things the same way?

- **Question Four:** Have I examined the benefits of making this sustainable investment (community/employee engagement, brand awareness, etc.)? How will this impact my business?
- **Question Five:** Do I have financing options to make this affordable right now? Is there someone or a business I can partner with to split the cost and usage with?

Let's compare two recent business cases.

Swire Beverages Ltd. is a Coca-Cola vendor in China. They provide bottles to the conglomerate and invest in water conservation. They aim to reduce water usage so that water consumed in the plant equals the volume of the beverage they produce. This includes the water used in processing their products, as well as cleaning in the bottling plant. In 2011, they reported a 39% reduction of water usage in their sustainability report. This represents billions of water saved in a country with a growing water crisis and significant financial savings. These water conservation measures are voluntary but are informed by backlash and regulation, fines, and other costs imposed on companies in the same industry.

Compare this to a bottler for Coca-Cola in India. They faced controversy and were forced to shut down for allegedly abusing water resources and contributing to a water shortage in the state of Kerala.

Swire is addressing an environmental obligation and, in doing so, are also minimizing a business risk. Water is a key resource not just to our survival, but to the survival of businesses, so it is wise for Swire to preserve its ongoing availability. This approach also improves Swire's business reputation, benefits the community, and allows continued operation.

These two stories show the importance of prioritizing environmental and social investment. Entrepreneurs and small businesses can reap the rewards of infusing their business practice and policies with environmental protection as a first priority. Often, entrepreneurs and small businesses can see *more* success with sustainable policies because the owner is actively involved with the business.

Five

Above and Beyond the Physical Environment

Sustainability in business is about more than just taking care of the environment. There are many other facets of sustainability that small businesses need to consider to remain competitive for the long term. These include managing company culture, valuing and investing in employees, and managing or engaging other stakeholders in your business. It's also important to support and nourish these relationships as they could make or break your business over time.

Personal relationships are key to small businesses and are also key to social innovation success. Smaller companies are likely to be more involved with their community, and employees will know each other and the owner quite well. When employees are considered family, which is more likely in smaller companies, the owner is more inclined to listen to employee concerns and involve them in the growth of the business. This can foster employee loyalty and decrease staff turnover, which is a huge cost-saver for any business. Staff training and recruitment is incredibly expensive, and any organization with high staff turnover is constantly frustrated with how much it costs their company. An easy fix is to treat your employees well, give them flexible hours and other benefits that they want, and your company will be rewarded with higher productivity and reduced staff costs in the long run.

Rather than considering payroll your biggest cost, as it often is when reported on the Income Statement, think of it as your greatest investment. The people who work for you are your greatest assets. Entrepreneurs tend to wear too many hats, but hopefully you've delegated a lot of those hats to qualified employees and rewarding them for doing so can help to future-proof your business. Building employee loyalty is just as important as building brand loyalty, as when an employee leaves, it costs up to 200% of their salary to replace them, depending on the position and level of specialized skills needed to do that job. This includes accounting for recruitment costs, training costs, and productivity losses. Less skilled work or entry-level positions earning under $30,000 will cost a company at least 16% of their salary to find and train a new employee. This percentage increases as you lose employees who are paid more and have important, specialized skills. Below is a graph of the median cost to replace employees (Centre for American Progress):

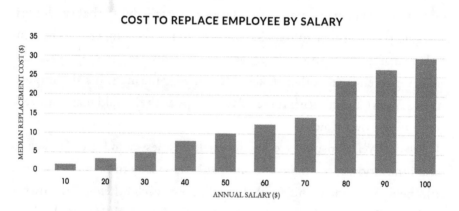

COST TO REPLACE EMPLOYEE BY SALARY

(y-axis: MEDIAN REPLACEMENT COST ($), x-axis: ANNUAL SALARY ($))

Figure 1 Graph displaying turnover costs (all figures in thousands)

It is important to keep in mind that studies like this are only able to measure the obvious, tangible effects of hiring a new employee, such as recruiting costs, training, and reduced productivity until the new employee is up to speed. Hidden costs, like remaining employee morale dropping as a result of turnover, also play a role. Other costs can include severance, paying out unused vacation days, and the administrative work of ensuring they have been removed from all employee authorization—not only things like being unable to enter your building anymore, but also removing them from group benefit plans so that they do not cost your company for benefits to which they are no longer entitled.

If you have a high turnover of staff, it is likely due to your workplace policies. Either there is a lack of career advancement opportunities, lack of intangible benefits, or lack of purpose for the employee to be engaged and excited about coming to work each day. Flexibility in the workplace is important to employees, especially millennials and parents who need to balance work and life commitments. Companies with a strong commitment to making their workforce happy have outperformed competitors.

Studies and reports have shown time and time again that it is advantageous for businesses to adopt this mindset, along with sustainable policies. In the coming years, these policies will be thrust upon business through regulation and other business obligations (e.g., case law and professional requirements). If a company is not already in line with these regulations and changes, it will be costly and time-consuming to change established business processes. It is always better for a business to implement an environmental policy that aligns with their values than be forced to conform to government policy.

In addition to measuring profit, you can also introduce performance indicators that measure employee and management happiness and productivity, customer satisfaction, and community engagement. Such measurements could include:

- Health of family relationships
- Enjoyment of work
- Physical health and well-being
- Level of satisfaction with life
- Opportunity for continued personal and professional development
- Having a meaningful livelihood that expresses passion, creativity, and soul
- Maintaining mental, physical, holistic spiritual health
- Having control over schedule
- Building interdependent web of life that provides an abundance of diverse perspectives and experiences

People are time-poor and happiness-poor. Rather than spending time with family and friends, or pursuing a hobby, they are spending more time commuting to their job.

Preventative care is always the least expensive health care option. Buying healthy food options may seem expensive, but not when you're borrowing from your future health. Plus, eating cheap junk food impairs your current health and productivity. Cancers, diseases, and illnesses can be a result of poor health that cost companies millions of dollars each year in lost productivity and sick days. Add to that the ongoing rising cost of health care, and spending an extra $5 a week on organic produce doesn't seem so bad.

Plan sustainability policies around your core business values and established brand, implementing what makes sense for your business. Communicate your intentions honestly with your customers and employees, and ask them to become involved to give you feedback and suggestions that you can evaluate and implement, if appropriate. This will avoid the potential greenwashing trap that can later damage a business's brand and customer loyalty. The last thing you want is for customers to feel that you've lied to them about your environmental efforts. Communication is key in becoming more sustainable, showing your customers that you also care about the issues they care about and are willing to listen to them to build a better business and leave the world better than when your business started.

These policies also centre around a common ideal, even if the initiatives vary wildly from company to company: use business as a force for good. This is the central ideal of the B Corp movement, which is essentially helping smaller companies quantify their impact on the world. This includes both good and bad impact, while providing suggestions on how to improve. Due to the vast differences between small businesses across different industries, the suggestions offered are catered well enough to suit any company while encompassing some universally accepted important sustainable benchmarks. This includes paying a living wage, offering parental leave to employees, access to health care, and assisting in saving for retirement. All of these things may be considered perks or benefits of a job, but realistically they are investments in your most valuable intangible asset: your workforce.

The Four Major Barriers to Successfully Implementing Sustainability

As entrepreneurs, we already have so much on our plate that part of the reason we're not doing more about our sustainable initiatives is because of too many responsibilities. In a constant state of competing priorities, how does business make the time to reap the financial rewards on the investment? And how do we give back to the communities that have supported us? That's what corporate social responsibility (CSR) is for. But there are a lot of reasons why it can be difficult to take that first step towards CSR.

TIME

To decrease time as a barrier, you need to be as efficient and impactful as possible. You must select the most ethical practices with the biggest impact for the least upfront cost, as noted in the carbon audit section. With little structure, you can have an effective green program that doesn't take much time to manage. Delegate the work by having a Green Champion in your office, either an intern or a colleague. Let them find solutions, empowering that employee. Allow yourself the final decision-making power of what to do, but the employee is responsible for integrating the solutions. You can also have an hour-long meeting once a month to keep everyone on track. When changing any habits, it takes commitment and time, and should be done slowly so that it sticks.

CASH

We've already busted the myth that sustainability is more expensive than business as usual. Often, a small business is cash-strapped, so investing in long-term projects and solutions is excused as too hard. The majority of cash barriers are actually behavioural and psychological. Many larger businesses evaluate the costs and benefits of implementing projects, including sustainable initiatives, to see how soon and how much of a benefit they would see from such an investment. This is an attitude small businesses must adopt towards sustainability, to find the low-hanging fruit that will yield quick results while planning to invest in longer-term projects that will have a larger impact on your business.

To help you get started, I would suggest that your business open a line of credit, if you don't have one already, to help pay for things as you need to, while you wait for money to flow back into your bank account. Even though change is a constant, it is still hard. It takes time, as noted above, and there is a learning curve. Remember when you started your business? It wasn't smooth sailing immediately. But with time, you created processes, infrastructure, efficiencies. These are the mentalities that need to be brought to new changes.

AUTHORITY

"I can't" is a common response. There are excuses like, "I don't own the building." But you can still improve leased spaces by adding plants known to improve indoor air quality or swapping out conventional flow taps for low-flow alternatives. You can also create flexibility for employees to work at home, work alternative hours (7 a.m. – 3 p.m. or 11 a.m. – 7 p.m.), or subsidise their use of public transit. What you need to acknowledge is that you have the power and the authority to implement change. If this is not something you have the time for, you have the authority to delegate the implementation of these initiatives to a passionate employee. So long as this person is given the autonomy and authority to make those changes, it will increase productivity and company loyalty. Not only do you have the power but you owe it to yourself, your employees, and the world.

KNOWLEDGE

Reading this book is a step in the right direction to achieve knowledge. Taking twenty minutes out of your day to do the Initial Quick B Corp Assessment is another quick thing you can do that could greatly increase your knowledge about where your business is compared to others, and what you can do moving forward. Sustainability can be a confusing endeavour for many because there is so much information out there. How do you know if it'll apply to you? Some websites to increase your baseline knowledge are:

- InHabitat.com
- DavidSuzuki.org
- GreenBiz.org
- SustainableBrands.com
- TreeHugger.com
- BCorporation.net

A sustainable business mentality needs to be embedded into all aspects of your business. It should be reflected in how you view your employees—as an investment in your company's future and productivity. It is also important to recognize the need to listen to what employees want and to provide that if you wish to retain top talent. Employees know when they are valued and heard, and will express their unhappiness in a variety of ways that hurt and cost your business.

While you may be resistant to this due to any of the barriers discussed above, empowering your employees to take on some of these initiatives will not just make them happier, but your business better.

SECTION II

I'M ON BOARD. WHERE DO I START?

Starting a business with environmental policies in place is great, as it will save you money throughout the life of your business. If you have an established business, you might be thinking, "Oh no, how much is it going to cost me to make these changes?"

No business is ever done improving. Integrating sustainability into the next phase of your improvement will only enhance your business. The saying that 'the best time to plant a tree was twenty years ago' applies here. It might have been best to start with sustainability when you began your business, but the next important day to start making a difference is today. Everything you do from this point will accumulate, and in a year's time, you'll be able to see that a change implemented had a measurable effect. This could be anything from reducing water usage to supporting local businesses to reducing fossil fuel consumption. This will translate to money saved, as well as building goodwill in your community. These savings and goodwill only grow with time. After two years, you'll have saved twice as much!

So I put to you to commit to doing three actions inspired by or within this book in your business or life:

1. A daily, simple practice
2. A mid-term goal that is a bit hard
3. A bigger goal to hit in twelve months' time

Treat this like any other business goal. For example, aim to increase revenue by X% or add Y offerings. This way, you are creating a daily habit of doing something good for the environment or your business, and you can feel immediate satisfaction, knowing you are making a small but accumulative difference. These are such things as starting a compost bin, eliminating single-use plastics in favour of washable utensils, minimizing water waste, sourcing your paper products from Forest Stewardship Council (FSC) suppliers, installing a programmable thermostat like EcoBee, etc.

The mid-term goal is a bit more challenging and needs more time to be implemented. It requires more planning or consistent action to complete. Such goals could include implementing a recycling program specific for your business, installing LED lights in your offices, etc.

The long-term goal is something you have to build towards and you can be creative with. Allow it to be specific to your situation and needs. It could be monitoring your carbon footprint and energy use for the year, committing to recording those numbers, and potentially offsetting it. Or it could be building a local community garden, compost centre, or farm. It might be joining or creating a mastermind group to be more effectively sustainable in your area. Becoming a leader in your community not only improves your standing among your peers, it also distinguishes your business. Many small businesses and entrepreneurs are inseparable from their personal lives. As many people want to be more environmentally conscious, you will show yourself to be a business that supports these values.

Six

"But What Can I Do?"
The Chapter of Hope

An important distinguishing factor in ethical entrepreneurship is that you and your business have already overcome the first, biggest hurdle: You care. Most large corporations struggle to implement social and environmentally-friendly business practices, where environmental and social responsibility take priority over profits, but many entrepreneurs start their business for these exact reasons.

Every single one of us has the choice and the ability to contribute to saving our planet. If every small business commits to plugging their electronics into an eco-efficient power bar, saving up to 500 kW per year, that equates to at least 50,000 kW in Canada alone, not to mention the energy lost on top of that in transmission from the power station to the outlet. This is because most businesses are small businesses, and our buying habits have the greatest impact of all. We decide to do things differently and, suddenly, we make the change we want to see a reality. When people say, "What can one person do?", the answer is actually a hell of a lot. The number of entrepreneurs or small business owners is between 27 and 55 million in the U.S. alone. If half of us change, think of the impact! Like interest, our actions compound on each other, gaining traction.

Part of the issue is that we like living the way we do. We are too comfortable with how we live, and change seems hard and bad. We think that structures put into place centuries ago can carry us into an ever-improving future. My friend, John Schrag, put it best: "If we had taken action to reduce emissions back in the 1980s when we first heard about climate change, the required action would have been very small, at approximately 2% reduction of emissions per year. It would have been relatively painless, and prevented any significant climate change. However, we did nothing for a long time, and, as a result, we are already feeling some effects of climate change. We will continue to experience these effects, even if we stop all carbon emissions today. Since we ignored those ten plus years of warnings, the best we can hope for now is to minimize the most catastrophic effects, and only through painful, expensive emissions cuts. It could have been cheap and painless, but that's not what we chose."

Be part of the movement. Here are things you can do to decrease your environmental footprint while decreasing the cost.

Fast and Easy

To start your journey, these are some easy ways that have significant results with little effort. Remember, though, to only replace these if necessary. The point is to upgrade appliances when replacing them, not create new waste by throwing everything away prematurely.

- Replace old lights with LED
- Add weather stripping and caulking to doors and windows
- Seal furnace ducts
- Replace your washing machine and only wash in cold water
- Install a programmable thermostat, like EcoBee
- Wrap water heater with an insulated blanket
- Replace your fridge
- Install a heat pump
- Replace your dishwasher
- Add insulation

Buying Based on Need

Consider the life cycle of impulse buys. Do you really need those cute sunglasses? Does the $10 price tag include the cost of disposal, air pollution, recycling manufacturing, and clean-up of the mining facilities or oil spills that may have occurred during extraction? If you stop buying things based on desire and focus more on need, it will decrease waste and clutter in your home and office.

The same goes for your business, whether it's buying products for your office or marketing materials to advertise your business. I've seen many businesses buy disposable items that are cheaply made but not particularly useful to the people receiving them. For example, USB sticks too small to hold anything of value, poor-quality tote bags, flyers and brochures, wristbands, lanyards, stickers. I'm sure you know of even more examples.

Watching the clean-up after any festival will reveal the enormous waste these products were to promote your business, as they are swept up into garbage trucks en route to the landfill. Instead, consider advertising in new or innovative ways that are useful to potential customers, reusable, and create a wider impact based on need.

Success Story: Beau's Brewery

A wonderful example of advertising your business through innovation and community impact is Beau's Brewery's Oktoberfest. Beau's Brewery is an Ontario-based B Corp that has had wide success across Canada with their sustainable, impact-based business. Their beer is made from organic, locally-grown hops. Their website lists their many impressive accomplishments, not the least of them being that they are Canada's largest organic craft brewery.

One of their sustainability initiatives was the Greener Futures Project, a member's only beer club that received exclusive beers. One-hundred percent of the revenue from this project (yes, revenue, not profits) funded green initiatives for their business. The first thing their Greener Futures Project paid for was their Bullfrog partnership, allowing Beau's to offset their electricity and natural gas use to become carbon neutral.

But Beau's didn't stop there. They also founded the Oktoberfest in their small town in 2008, which has grown into one of the largest Oktoberfests in southern Ontario, where all the money raised goes to charity. Beau's CEO, Steve Beauchesne, said that Board members at the company question why Beau's doesn't keep that money for themselves, using the success of the event as an additional income stream for the business. Instead of viewing the cost of the event as charity and the donations as lost profit, Beau's views the event as an advertising expense. Rather than spending that $100,000 elsewhere on marketing, by creating a community event they are advertising to the many thousands of people in attendance. Beauchesne said, "Traditionally, business people are more comfortable spending money on advertising than on a community event, even if the end results are the same in terms of brand awareness and increased sales. For us, Beau's Oktoberfest is a way to create an event that we want and also help others with the money we raise. And because these funds would not exist without this event, for us it justifies continuing to run it and make it better each year."

This advertising model is innovative because it breaks traditional business rules. As a business, you expect to make money from the activities your business pursues. Advertising, on the other hand, is an expense intended to create brand awareness and potential customers. Beau's turns this around and makes a charitable business activity into a way to raise brand awareness. The risk is similar—spend money to potentially gain customers—but we feel more comfortable with the traditional advertising model, despite the many benefits that come from Beau's approach.

At its essence, Beau's Oktoberfest is a vehicle to raise money. While Beau's is technically giving away that money, it would not have manifested without the initial fundraising efforts. This is justification enough for Beau's to donate the funds, since they would not have raised them otherwise. This approach is fascinating and innovative, included in a business model where they are transparent, allowing their clients to contribute through product purchasing and know the impact of their purchase.

Recycle

Words of caution: Beware of the recycling trap. A solopreneur or small business can make a far greater impact on their waste management by not buying things in the first place. Refuse to buy items with excessive packaging, and choose to reuse plastic containers instead of recycling them.

Technically, there is no such thing as recycling, just down-cycling. This means plastics put in the recycling bin are taken for processing. Often, processing means being melted down into products that are of a lesser quality or lower structure than the original item. This process is extremely energy-intensive and not ideal for ethical businesses to work towards. We should be focused more on reducing our waste entirely, reusing as much as possible, and refusing to buy items where possible. The less material that goes into the waste system, the more environmentally-friendly your business will be.

Benefits of recycling include saving energy, preventing greenhouse gas emissions, conserving natural resources for future generations, creating jobs, and providing valuable raw materials for industry. By recycling and composting, you can lower your garbage collection bill, especially in communities that charge by the bag.

If your main waste service provider doesn't recycle, then you may need an additional provider to maximize waste diversion. However, more services equal more costs, so it's important to reduce waste as much as possible.

Material that can be recycled, depending on your local garbage and recycling centres:

- Organic material, like wood or tissue paper
- Paper and cardboard
- Hard and soft plastics
- Metal
- Glass
- Cartons and paper cups
- Foil bags and wrappers
- Styrofoam
- Batteries

Waste Not, Want Not

Cradle to Cradle made an excellent point that waste is what businesses, and people, don't have a use for. One person's trash is another person's treasure is a great mentality when thinking of waste. While you may not have a use for it, someone else may. However, avoiding waste in the first place is more efficient.

Waste management tips:
- Avoid disposable crockery and cutlery
- Avoid single-use milks and sugars
- Restrict paper towel use to one roll every two weeks
- Cater only as much food as needed for meetings and office parties. If there are leftovers, encourage staff or attendees to take them home.
- Discourage paper waste by not buying a printer. If your office is small, it is more cost effective to go to Staples or OfficeMax when you have to print a batch of reports. Also, this will make you and your staff think twice before printing!
- Contact TerraCycle to buy one of their all-waste bins and divert your waste to a recycling supplier
- Ask suppliers to minimize packaging or take back packaging to reuse
- Avoid over-ordering supplies and raw materials, especially those with a short shelf life

The last tip is particularly important, as there is an extraordinary amount of unnecessary waste in North America from over-buying products that are not needed and then go to waste because they spoil. This is a costly exercise for your business, so avoid wasting your money altogether by only buying what you need or what you will use.

Many items on the above list are disposable. A great way to reduce waste drastically *and* save money is to replace these disposable items with ones that are much longer-term. For example, using rags for the majority of messes instead of paper towels or a solid razor instead of disposable razors. All of these little incremental disposable costs add up to a lot, as Chelsea Fagan from

The Financial Diet explains multiple times in her videos: "Whatever your [disposable] habit happens to be, it's important to get out of the disposal mentality wherever possible. Generally speaking, a disposable product just means costing you more money for a little bit of convenience."

She mentions just a few of the products that are high on waste with costs that add up if you continuously use them. Some of the many items this includes are:

- Razors
- Paper towels
- Travel-sized accessories
- Chopsticks
- Sweeping cloths
- Non-rechargeable batteries
- Sandwich bags
- Single-serve coffee pods
- Cling wrap
- Single-use stir sticks
- Disposable cups for drinks

A great way to find out your disposable kryptonite is to do a zero-waste challenge for 30 days. There are multiple places online where you can sign up for a free zero-waste challenge that will show you ways to minimize waste and offer tips along the way.

Paper

Six ways to rethink paper use in the office:

1. Decrease the amount of paper you use but also question your type of paper. Ask your suppliers the following questions:
   - What is the recycled content of the paper?
   - How is the product shipped?
   - Is the paper Forest Stewardship Council (FSC) certified?
2. Ask staff about opportunities to save paper. Generate ideas and assign responsibility to implement them.

3. Consider changing office processes and activities to limit or eliminate paper-intensive practices.
4. Move to a paperless editing system. Track changes or other functions can be effective and efficient to draft, review, and finalize documents.
5. Encourage paperless meetings in your office. Send agendas electronically and use a projector or whiteboard to show the agenda and review documents with staff.
6. Utilize paperless payment systems to reduce money spent on postage, envelopes, and time.

File sharing, employing electronic practices for surveys, forms, and invoices, and scanning paper documents can reduce long-term waste. Eliminating the need to print is one of the easiest and most cost-saving efforts.

Paper can also be repurposed before it is recycled. Collect single-sided, non-confidential paper, and find ways to reuse it. They can be made into notebooks, reused for single-sided documents, or even used in an art project. Envelopes can be used for making lists or notes or relabeling file folders.

The final place for paper is in the recycling bin. If paper is soiled, then it can go into the compost. Ask your landlord about recycling and, if not included, put it in future lease agreements or ask your local municipality about options.

Other paper office products, like stationary and file hangers, all have an environmental impact. Considering doing without. For those you need, get environmentally-certified brands and ask your supplier if they recycle stationary, so you can return products at the end of their life. Ask providers what kind of criteria they use to label their products as being 'green'. Greener may cost more, but they will often last longer, which will save you money.

Starting a green purchasing policy that includes a checklist for things you buy helps to adhere to environmental values in daily purchasing decisions. Perhaps this is too formal in a small office, but it can be highly effective to put your purchasing guidelines in writing and ensure people are following procedures that align with your green principles.

Have a set of sustainable preferable criteria for common products that you purchase. It's not enough for a supplier to say they're green. Products should be certified by an independent third party like ECOLOGO, Green Seal, FSC, etc. Other things you could include as part of your supplier purchasing policy include:

- Recycled content more than 50%
- Preference given to women-owned or majority women-owned businesses
- Purchasing from suppliers that use minimal packaging or accept returns of their packaging for reuse
- Companies are in compliance with all local laws and regulations, including social or environmental performance
- Good governance policies are made public, including policies related to ethics and corruption
- Demonstrating above-regulation standards for things like environmentally-friendly manufacturing process, excellent labour practices, minimal land or water usage, etc.
- Third-party certifications related to positive social and/or environmental performance

You can ask for this information informally, or you can draft a supplier survey questionnaire to send to your suppliers to fill in. When doing so, it is important to explain why you are asking for this information. This could be because you want to work with suppliers that have implemented certain standards as a part of your mission statement, or because you are looking to understand your suppliers better and manage your relationship with them. The idea is to understand their business better, not to increase your paperwork or theirs.

Clean Yes, Germs No: Eco-Friendly Cleaning Products

Eco-friendly cleaning products are important for employees on a variety of fronts. Commercial cleaners are harmful to skin, irritate eyes, and can impact the respiratory system. Volatile organic compounds (VOCs) are found in everyday cleaning products, become airborne, and enter our skin and lungs. This can cause headaches, skin irritations, and dizziness. Also, high concentrations or long-term exposure cause chronic diseases and cancer. This is what you and your staff are being exposed to on a regular basis. This is particularly important if your office is located in a building with little to no ventilation, or the building had an indoor air quality test done that was sub-par. Sick building syndrome has been an increasing issue since the 1970s due to lower ventilation standards, according to the EPA, and negatively impacts your workers and their productivity.

Switching to green cleaning solutions reduces toxic exposure and improves air quality. Look for products that are:

- Low in VOCs
- Biodegradable
- Nontoxic
- Free of carcinogens, mutagens, and asthmagens
- Free of petroleum-based ingredients
- Concentrated, so you can dilute them yourself
- Made of recycled content and packaging
- Locally sourced, to reduce transport costs and carbon emissions
- Not in aerosol cans

Some homemade recipes, like water and vinegar for window cleaner, are significantly cheaper than what is commonly used. Baking soda as an air freshener is another example. You can easily add essential oils for a refreshing smell, and all the ingredients are compostable. Using a natural air freshener also eliminates synthetic fragrances, which is becoming a more common sensitivity and allergy. It's no surprise, considering fragrances and air fresheners frequently contain formaldehyde and benzene, a known neurotoxin. Hand soap can also be replaced with castile soap, filtered water, and, if desired, essential oils. My personal soap preference is Seventh Generation, a company on a mission to decrease their carbon footprint.

By decreasing toxins in the environment, you are decreasing health risks. This means fewer sick days and higher productivity.

Business Clothing: Eco-fashion

Have you ever spent over $100 on a dress or fancy outfit for a special occasion and then never worn it again? What do you do with these dresses? Donate them to a second-hand store, I hope.

Did you know that you also have another option? Dress and formal occasion rentals have been exploding in the last few years because you're able to rent a dress for the night or weekend, for a fraction of the price of purchase. Return it when you're done so that it's not taking up valuable space in your closet!

Plus, next time you have another gala to attend, you can go and rent an entirely new dress and continue to look as gorgeous and fabulous as you are. It's about time this service was widely available, because men have been able to rent their tuxedos rather than paying exuberant prices for their own suit that they may wear once or twice per year. This way, you spend a fraction on your clothing and you'll always be in fashion. In that way, you're like a celebrity!

Food for Thought: Catering and Food Products

An easy way to decrease your indirect emissions in company catering is to increase the availability of vegetarian options. I recommend increasing the percentage of vegetarian offerings at a buffet-style company event to 50%. This is the minimum if you have vegetarians or vegans attending the event, as meat-eaters are likely to graze on vegetarian foods, reducing the amount of vegetarian food available. A lack of options could mean the vegetarians are unable to eat enough and will feel undervalued and unappreciated. It is not enough to order 20% vegetarian if 20% of your attendees are vegetarian. The only exception to this is if each attendee is being served an individualized meal.

It is also wise to consider catering options that support the local economy or who are helping under-served populations. A local Toronto caterer and B Corp, Paintbox, works to provide employment opportunities to the local neighbourhood, where residents face many barriers to employment and training. Their initiatives help lift up these residents and provide them with meaningful work and is at the core of their mission as a company. There is likely a similar caterer in your area, or one who has a particular focus on environmental practices. You can find out by asking some basic questions.

Questions to ask your caterer:

1. Do you source local, seasonal, organic products?
2. Does your company recycle and compost all food waste?
3. Do you have reusable dishes (china, linen, etc.)?
4. Do you offer compostable cups, napkins, and cutlery?
5. Do you source eco-friendly meat and seafood (free range, organic, Ocean Wise)?
6. Can you supply juices and water in pitchers instead of individual cans or bottles?
7. Can you supply sugar, cream, jams, and other condiments in bowls or jars instead of single-serve packages?
8. Do you serve certified Fair Trade and organic coffee and teas?

Electronics

Most offices are dependent on electronics. From computers and printers to fridges and vacuum cleaners, we use a lot of gadgets to keep our businesses running smoothly. The type of electronics you use should always be energy efficient. One of the easiest, cheapest, and most cost effective ways to decrease your power usage is an energy efficient power bar. It can decrease your energy needs by 67 kW a year per device, almost a third of its energy use in a year. When plugged in, electronics can cause phantom loads—the equipment pulling energy despite not using it. An energy efficient power bar reduces this drain. Anything plugged in can have a drain, but here is an incomplete list to spark your imagination: stereos, phone chargers, fax machines, printers, copy machines, phones with displays, coffee machines with displays, microwaves, scanners, mailing machines, laptop chargers, battery chargers, etc.

We will get more into this during the energy audit but understanding your energy usage as well as when and why there are spikes, allows you to then reduce the spikes. Here is an example of a breakdown, to see common energy demands.

Equipment Type	Wattage (W)	Quantity	Monthly Operating Hours	Monthly Power Usage
Printers	400 watts	5	40	80,000 watts

Ways to reduce energy:
- Turn off printers at night to reduce standby power use
- Use printers less frequently, which also helps to conserve paper
- Reduce number of printers
- Begin replacing printers with more efficient models

Computers	300 watts	20	160	960,000 watts

Ways to reduce energy:
- Turn off computers when not in use, even for 10 minutes
- Replace monitors with high efficient LCD versions
- Replace desktop computers with laptops
- Use power saving modes to reduce energy consumption of each computer

Table 1 Electronic Energy Usage

Notice that a lot of these suggestions are behavioural changes? By changing behaviour, you can save between 5% and 20% in energy costs. Plus, it costs very little to implement.

You can also buy renewable energy certificates from a variety of sources to offset energy usage if you cannot source energy from renewable and local sources.

Energy

There are three steps to sustainable energy consumption:

1. Reduction or elimination,
2. Renewable energy generation, and
3. Offsetting energy consumed.

As a general rule, the most sustainable action to take is to first see where waste can be eliminated. This also applies to energy. Where are you wasting energy?

MONEY SAVING DEVICE: If your office powers a lot of devices, use a TrickleStar eco power bar. They're excellent for a home office and the home. These power bars reduce energy drain from idling appliances or electronics on standby. You probably need to buy a power bar, so why not buy one that's going to save you money while being incredibly useful at the same time?

Depending on your business, this could be any number of things. Do you have the most efficient machinery or technology? Are you using the technology or equipment in the most efficient way possible? Is it possible to not leave it idling? Is your tech or equipment turned off when not in use for extended periods of time? Does your company operate nine-to-five, during high-peak energy consumption hours? Can you offer flexible hours to employees who want to come in earlier and leave earlier? Or in contrast, start later and leave later, so that some of your energy consumption is off-peak hours? Encourage using battery-powered devices during the day (e.g., encourage employees to unplug laptops), using their charge while energy prices are at their peak. Encourage installing updates at night and turning off computers overnight.

Does your office building over-air-condition or over-heat? Survey or ask your employees this question and observe whether they are leaving doors or windows open unnecessarily to let the air or heat escape. This may be a sign that your business is wasting money to heat or cool a building too much. If stock needs to be kept at a certain temperature, isolate and insulate it to prevent excess energy costs.

HOT TIP: During the summer, shut the curtains on south- and west-facing windows. Your rooms will be an average of five degrees warmer with the curtains open, meaning any air conditioning will work 50 times harder to keep the space cool.

MONEY SAVING DEVICE: EcoBee is another fantastic money and energy saving device. It connects to your home heating/air conditioning unit and allows you to set a schedule so that the heat/air turns off when you're not home. This saves you money by eliminating waste and can be programmed to turn on 30 minutes prior to you arriving home. You can also program it to increase the temperature during the night. As your body cools down, your bedroom is maintained at a comfortable temperature rather than being tangled in blankets! It also syncs with your smartphone, allowing you to make on-the-spot changes in case you come home early, late, or go away on an extended vacation. It's a great product that earns its return on investment within the first month of use!

Encouraging a casual dress code during the summer can be another way to reduce energy consumption. Japan has encouraged the 'casual salesman' dress code for decades, allowing men to don more weather-appropriate clothing than a three-piece suit. This means buildings are cooled to more moderate temperatures, and people are not sweating through too many layers in the summer.

Another potential area of waste is corporate travel. This would mean investing in teleconferencing and telecommuting, but this is becoming the norm in most companies. It is a great way to decrease your carbon footprint, and keep your employees happy—a win-win! If I haven't covered something that may be relevant in your business, ask the people around you and listen to their suggestions. Your employees probably have great ideas on how your business can reduce its energy needs. Your friends and business mentors probably have great suggestions, possibly from personal experience. Ask them and see what they have to say and how you can implement those suggestions into your business.

Moving on to renewables, this is when you look at converting your current energy usage to renewable options. It is important to do this step AFTER reducing your energy usage as much as possible. When I interviewed Bruce Taylor, founder of Enviro-Stewards, to learn from his extensive sustainability wisdom, one of his major pieces of advice to businesses is to reduce waste wherever possible. Taylor said, "There's no use in jumping into building solar panels and windmills before assessing if your factory is wasting energy. Then you're just wasting solar energy instead of your local grid's energy. The most important step to any sustainability effort is to reduce first; it is the step that will make the biggest bottom line impact."

This philosophy and approach to sustainability is critical to increasing profit through changes in business practices. I've said it before and I'll say it again, waste reduction is the fastest way to decrease your environmental footprint and fastest way to increase profit.

That is not to say renewable energy is not important—it is absolutely critical and necessary for society to move towards renewables for our energy needs. However, there is much we can do in our business and personal lives to save energy and money, which will allow us to make more informed, and therefore better, choices about moving to renewable energy.

Though if your company is interested in installing solar panels or wind turbines, I want to encourage you to do that. It may be one of your longer-term goals, but it's also great if it's a short-term goal. Many local and state governments are offering support to feed renewables into our energy grid, often offering grants or tax credits to install them. Be sure to include these credits or grants in your calculation when reviewing and comparing the costs and benefits of installing them.

Finally, offset energy through carbon credits or with a similar program. For some businesses, especially in the foreseeable future, it is not feasible to install solar or wind power. But if you still want to be carbon neutral, enter carbon offsetting from stage right. This is the process of paying an external company through a carbon credit program, which may be from a private company or a government program depending on your local and industry situation. A private company might be one like Bullfrog Power that builds low impact renewable energy and helps to finance solar and wind farms across Canada. This feeds renewable energy into the grid, so while you aren't installing your own renewable energy, you are contributing to creating more sustainable energy overall.

Now, you are probably wondering how spending money on making your business carbon neutral increases profit. Yes, doing this may increase your expenses slightly. However, the marketing benefits outweigh that incremental cost if you want to prove to skeptical consumers that you are building a more sustainable business. Also, it will future-proof your business for the long-term, when being carbon neutral is a regulated requirement. Would your business be ready for that? Would you know how to report and calculate what it would take to be carbon neutral? It is much better to be prepared for such a regulation change, rather than be reactionary. It will save a lot of money and time in years to come.

Below are some resources and companies to consider to offset carbon. This is by no means an extensive list, as offsetting carbon can take many forms, from planting trees in the Amazon to investing in local composting programs. For example, Shopify is investing in carbon sequestering programs that are up to twenty times more expensive than carbon credits, but this is part of their mandate as a company, to have a positive environmental impact and increase the demand of carbon sequestration efforts.

Calculating and Buying Carbon Credits

BUYING RENEWABLE ENERGY CERTIFICATES (RECs)

Also known as 'green tags', this is a great way to offset your energy usage, if putting up your own solar panels or wind turbine isn't an option—which, let's face it, isn't an option for most businesses. But by doing this, you are helping to accelerate a green-powered grid, as the partnership exists to expand the use of access to solar energy. Here is just one example: www.energy.gov/eere/solar/national-community-solar-partnership

BULLFROG POWER (CANADA)

Bullfrog Power is a service to offset your home or business's electricity. They ensure the energy put on the grid on your behalf is from clean, low-impact, renewable sources. Learn more at bullfrogpower.com

LESS EMISSIONS (CANADA)

A sister company to Bullfrog Power, Less was born out of a need to give Canadians a way to offset their air-travel-related emissions. You can also use it to buy carbon offsets by the tonne, if you've already calculated your emissions and need an easy way to offset them. Learn more at less.ca

These companies have been certified by an external auditor to ensure they meet 'The Gold Standard', so you can trust that your money is going into efforts to reduce carbon emissions. Other companies include Carbonzero (carbonzero.ca), CarbonX (carbonx.ca), and TerraPass (terrapass.com/carbon-footprint-calculator).

There will likely be ones locally you could purchase carbon credits from as well. Make sure to check that your government doesn't have a carbon credit trading program in place, as that will also be a viable place to purchase.

Fuel for Thought: Coffee Machines and Ancillary Products

It is the fuel for late night brainstorming sessions, the reason we get up in the morning, and the driving force to get us through difficult times. So, let's go green with our black coffee. Here are a few changes to make coffee not just good for your team but good for the earth.

What kind of coffee machine do you use? No-filter drip machines and French presses are low in waste and the coffee grinds make for excellent, nutrient-rich mulch for most office plants. If you're determined to use a single-use cartridge coffee machine, be sure to TerraCycle the cartridges. You can also buy reusable cartridges for your work coffee machine to fill with ground coffee.

Other environmental changes:
- Compost coffee grinds and tea bags
- Stir coffee and tea with spoons instead of plastic or wooden sticks
- Avoid single-serve packets of sugar, milk, and cream
- Choose local, organic sugar and cream
- Turn off machines at night and when not in use

All of the above will decrease waste and will save you money over the long run.

Be sure to buy coffee and tea that is fair trade. This can easily be done by buying from a local coffee shop that makes their own teas and roasts their own coffee. Otherwise, be sure the coffee is Rainforest Alliance Certified™, UTZ certified, or Bird Friendly®.

Hand Dryer

The most sustainable way to dry hands is with energy efficient hand dryers because of the grander shift to renewable energy sources. The electricity used by modern hand dryers is quite small compared to the energy used in the production and distribution of paper towels. You can search for 'Energy Efficient Hand Dryers' to see what is available in your area. Dyson Airblades are popular because they are slim and effective, but compare the options available. Based on your priorities, cost-per-use may be more important to consider, but there are many choices available. However, if you currently use paper towels, throw them in the compost. Consider using reusable cloth hand towels, if water is not scarce in your community. It is common in Japan, where there are no paper towels or hand dryers, for everyone to carry a small hand towel in their purse or pocket.

Landscaping

Appropriate landscaping can be a saver on many fronts. The first is maintenance and water. If you select plants native to your area, it will decrease the amount of water you'll need because they are acclimatized to the current water provided; they have a higher chance of survival, which decreases the chance that you will need to replace them; and they are usually cheaper.

Change the Way You Commute

The time has come to change the way we drive. Michelle Conlin in her article, "Extreme Commuting", outlines the harsh toll we pay for commuting. In addition to gas use, congestion, pollution, and urban sprawl, there are also physical consequences like high blood pressure, musculoskeletal disorders, increased hostility, and lateness. This is not the way to start a day and it surely has an impact on worker performance. In *Bowling Alone: The Collapse and Revival of American Community*, author Robert D. Putnam believes that every 10 minutes of commuting cuts one's social connections by 10%. This is a huge loss of time that could be spent with family, friends, and oneself. Distance commuted also impacts divorce rates. Still, people are spending long periods of time commuting. The U.S. Department of Energy estimates that 51% of household gas emissions are from commuting. 51%! This isn't even considering the impact from the infrastructure of commuting. The heat island effect, which increases heat in cities due to concrete and pavement that absorb heat, in combination with the heat created by cars and then air conditioners being cranked because of said heat, illustrates that the environment we've created due to cars is ludicrous. To say we need to change the way we commute is an understatement; we need to revolutionize it.

Switching to a hybrid car is an excellent long-term investment, especially if you are unable to change your current driving habits in the next few years for various reasons. However, the larger cost savings is to get rid of your car altogether. In the interim, changing your driving habits is the starting point.

- Switch to biking, public transportation where available, or carpooling with neighbours for anything from grocery shopping to your work commute.
- If a car is needed for errands, string together multiple ones that need car access to decrease impact.
- Locate your office close to where your employees live or in a central location to decrease commuting times.
- Do not drive above the speed limit. A car delivery company saved one billion annually when they mandated their drivers go 63 mph rather than 65 mph.
- Educate your employees with driver education to ensure maximum efficiency when driving.
- Decrease idling time to decrease wasted fuel.
- Offer employees rides home, via taxi or ride-share apps, in case of emergency.

Commuting is a good example of where environmental restrictions are being applied and influencing daily life. In London, England, Mayor Ken Livingstone imposed a congestion tax to enter the city centre commencing in 2003. As people switched to public transit, cycling, walking, and carpooling, 50,000 fewer vehicles entered the city daily. Traffic speeds increased, transit service became faster and more reliable, accidents were reduced, noise and pollution levels decreased, and the city found a new source of revenue to invest in sustainable transportation. In Toronto, Canada, a portion of a busy street has banned cars to facilitate public transportation and increase foot traffic. As we move ahead, changes like these will become more frequent to deal with gridlock and pollution.

But you should also be the change you want to see in the world. Invest your money in alternative commuting methods.

Water

As an Australian, water waste has always boggled my mind. As the population grows, we will continue to deplete our clean water sources. Water costs are rising due to access, but the price will continually increase as storms worsen from climate change. Water will become contaminated by sewage and other toxins leaking into the drinking supply.

The first course of action is to acknowledge we must change our behaviour. Here are simple things you can do immediately to reduce water consumption:

- If your business doesn't operate 24/7, check the overnight or downtime consumption, as it will often detect leaks and other problems.
- Identify opportunities for water recovery. Often taps are turned on and left with water running right down the drain. If you are doing dishes, consider plugging the sink and reusing the water to wash all your dishes (cleanest to dirtiest) rather than leaving water running the entire time. This will save approximately $3 per load of dishes.
- Considering reusing water where possible. Collect grey shower water and redirect it to flush your toilet or clean your car. Clean your car with a bucket and sponge rather than with a hose.

- Reduce the amount of grass on your office or home lawn. Grass consumes an unnecessary amount of clean, drinkable water. If you must have grass, consider watering it with grey water.
- Replace grass with native plants and flowers. Consider growing an herb and fruit garden for your employees to enjoy the fruits of their labour.
- Install dual flush or low flush toilets. If that isn't an option right now, make sure to install dual flush when you need to replace your toilet. In the interim, adjust your toilet float to save money. You can also put a gallon jug of water or a brick in your toilet to reduce the amount of water being flushed each time. This could save you $1 per flush or $120 per month. This could save you 16% on your water bill if you have an old-style, 16-gallon flush toilet.
- Purchase a water-conserving dishwasher.
- Make sure there is a procedure to fix water leaks as soon as possible and communicate this with your staff.
- Install trigger nozzles on any hoses in the office or at home.

Be aware that as storms become increasingly worse, water waste treatment regulations will also become more stringent and costly, adding to the price of water. If local government can afford to spare the resources, they will need to increase testing of those waters as flooding can cause sewage to leak into streams and the drinking supply. Any local governments cutting costs on water treatment would want to remember Flint, Michigan. Their water crisis began in 2014. Widespread media coverage has made the crisis a household name, plus multiple criminal and civil lawsuits have reinforced the importance of prioritizing access to clean water over lowering costs incrementally.

Transition to Be a LEED Building

LEED (Leadership in Energy and Environmental Design) is the most widely used U.S. standard for certifying green buildings. The rating system provides guidelines related to design, construction, and operation of buildings. If transitioning your buildings to be LEED-certified isn't possible, you can be inspired by their standards to include some great alterations to make your office more engaging and worker friendly.

Think it's more expensive? Think again. Despite the common myth that a green building costs more, green buildings have minimal or no additional construction costs, but do reduce your operating costs over its life. Numerous examples prove that green building can be cost-effective in various facets of your business.

The facts: Poor indoor air quality is a serious health problem. Annually, millions of people in the U.S. are affected by sick building syndrome. Workers might experience fatigue, difficulty concentrating, and irritated eyes as a result of poor ventilation, mould, chemical exposure, and poor lighting.

Protecting productivity: Designing buildings is beyond the scope of this book, but here are some guidelines to keep in mind in conversations with architects, facility managers, or leasing agents.

- Choose construction materials and interior finish products with zero or low emissions (VOCs) to improve indoor air quality.
- Provide adequate ventilation. Building codes generally have minimum rates of ventilation, but green buildings usually exceed these rates. Ventilation systems can be mechanical or passive. Some buildings have CO_2 sensors that set ventilation systems into action to optimize the oxygen levels inside.
- Keep air intakes away from exhaust areas! Surprisingly, this common sense, but often overlooked, design guideline is a common cause of Sick Building Syndrome.
- Provide adequate filtration. Install ventilation systems with devices that take harmful particulates and pollutants out of the air.
- Prevent indoor mould through selection of materials resistant to microbial growth and control humidity.
- Enable occupants to control their environment by installing operable windows and personal workstation climate controls. A University of California, Berkeley study shows that workers are more comfortable when they can control their workplace temperature, as they can turn off unnecessary air conditioning or heating.

- Ensure that maintenance crews use non-toxic cleaning materials because many cleaning products are caustic or emit gases, such as VOCs and formaldehyde, that impact health and well-being. Start with your own purchasing department. Whether they buy supplies for your maintenance crew or contracts with an outside janitorial service, request—or insist—that they use nontoxic or green cleaning supplies. Find certified products, including safe cleaning materials, paints, and finishes, at Green Seal.
- Before signing a lease, verify whether the building was constructed using nontoxic materials and whether the common area cleaning service uses green supplies.
- Include health concerns and indoor air quality in the building commissioning process. Be sure to request post-construction testing to make sure heating, air conditioning, and lighting systems work properly and efficiently.

This list isn't exhaustive. There are so many things, little to enormous, that you can do to make the world a slightly better place. There is nothing too small or too large when it comes to the environment and making changes.

Seven

Environmental Business Successes

Turning your passion into a profitable, sustainable business isn't just a fad; it's the centre of the current wave of entrepreneurs building multi-million-dollar companies. The influx of organic, fair trade products at the grocery store or many paper products sporting the FSC logo is just the surface of changes occurring. There are buildings proudly displaying their LEED certification and businesses proudly showcasing their environmental accolades and how they improve the lives of their employees, customers, and suppliers. This is all while protecting the environment. Folks are leaving the corporate world, tired of the questionable ethics, to start their own companies and are doing so with an intent to do good in the world.

Purpose-driven business is booming. Solar energy is a growing market that's creating millions of jobs in North America, nutrition coaches are in high demand to empower their clients to be healthier while being mindful of the planet. Kombucha is a perfect example of this new wave. Increasingly popular in North America, kombucha originated in Europe. According to Mintel, a global market research company, the European markets of Spain, Poland, and France, are seeing more than 50% of consumers seeking alternatives to bubbly drinks. They seek beverages with natural ingredients, that are healthier than traditional drinks. This trend includes other niches, as Carly Stein, the founder of Beekeeper's Naturals, discovered.

Success Story: Beekeeper's Naturals

Carly Stein built a successful company on sustainable principles from day one. Stein's business was born out of her antibiotics allergy. Growing up, she spent a lot of time and money looking for natural alternatives but didn't find any that worked. While living in Italy, she developed tonsillitis but had the good fortune to walk into a pharmacy that recommended propolis, a beehive by-product. She tried it and found that it worked. Throughout her European travels, Stein found that propolis was a fairly common substance that many people knew about and would recommend for all sorts of infections as an alternative to antibiotics.

No one was selling propolis in North America, so when Stein returned home, she had to develop her own spray, which would become her flagship product. In doing so, she also discovered an untapped market. Beekeeper's Naturals is a huge advocate for beekeeping in a way that nourishes bee populations, garnering respect with retailers and customers early on. For example, Stein didn't use just any beekeepers. Because bees can forage up to five miles (or eight kilometres) away, the bees, and their products, can be contaminated by pesticides used on neighbouring farms. To retain the high quality, Stein worked with beekeepers in remote locations, far from farms who use pesticides, so as not to infect the hive. Pesticides are the number one threat to bee populations right now. Once customers began to see real benefits from the propolis spray, heightened by the purity, they became advocates for the product.

As her company flourished, Stein faced the challenge of growing too quickly and, at one point, there wasn't enough raw product to meet demand. She had a difficult choice: break her supply chain of working exclusively with sustainable beekeepers, retaining the quality of the product, or place folks on back-orders. Stein chose the latter, to be out of stock for a period of time. This was a defining moment for her and her company, choosing to potentially lose business or anger important retailers in favour of protecting bees and the integrity of her business. It also meant Beekeeper's Naturals had to educate retailers and their distributors about the importance of quality and avoiding tainted supplies. Bees rely on honey for their own food and many beekeepers over harvest the hives by taking all the honey for retail purposes, feeding the bees sugar water instead of letting them take care of themselves. Taking the time to educate retailers allowed them to repair their business relationships and showcase that Beekeeper's Naturals was a company that stood by its value to protect bee populations.

Stein deliberately broke the number one rule for a burgeoning company: Do not go out of stock. Sourcing inferior raw ingredients was at odds with the company's mission, one that resonated with the employees, and that action could have resulted in significant employee turnover costs. Also, an inferior product could be seen as a betrayal by returning clients, who are critically important to the continued existence of a young business. It is far more costly to have to continually find new customers than it is to have a reliable repeat customer base.

As experts in bees and sustainable beekeeping, Stein and her team readily share their knowledge with new partners, retailers, customers, and suppliers. This collaboration strengthened their supply chain, through loyalty and demand, but has also future-proofed their company to ensure that Beekeeper's Naturals will always have quality raw products. And as Beekeeper's Naturals says, Mother Nature knows best. It should have been obvious that bees were the answer to natural alternatives all along.

Eight

By the Numbers

Measuring Your Impact and Why It's Important

'If you can't measure it, you can't manage it' applies to your business's environmental impact. When you measure your business's environmental impact, you are able to see where you currently stand within your own guidelines and against other businesses in your industry. Plus, you can then identify low hanging fruit for your business to begin to improve on.

A successful business measures what's most important to it, which doesn't have to stop at revenue, profit, or growth. Ethical businesses should include more than just bottom line numbers, because they don't always include things that are important to your company. For example, if you want your business to reduce its waste footprint, finding out how much garbage, recycling, and organic waste your business produces is essential. A waste audit will show you how many cubic metres/tons of garbage is going to the landfill each year.

Accounting for the Environment

"A bee doesn't send you an invoice for pollinating a flower. And yet they are critical to a trillion-dollar global industry."
— Pavan Sukhdev, "Put a Value on Nature", TED Talk

Accounting and finance are shifting to measure and mitigate the true risks and costs of business from environmental impact to exploitation of vulnerable communities. These practices have historically been excluded from accounting, which only measured within the binary of debit and credit. Basically, recording only what it costs to create a product or service, and how much they receive in selling that product or service. But you know there are hidden costs and benefits, depending on the business, that require accounting with a sustainability focus. Carbon markets attempt to account for this, but they are only focused on one aspect of a business's activities. They're a step in the right direction, but only a step.

We must expand the definitions of accounting and what it includes to our business externalities in a way that is currently missing. Modern accounting is myopically profit-focused and, as a result, deeply flawed. We don't really know how to take everything into account. Businesses don't merely lose valuable information because of this disconnect from reality—they are literally blind to opportunities that the income statement and balance sheet currently cannot recognize.

Increasingly, companies are being required to track and disclose environmental risks, performance, and usage as a part of their annual financials statements. Various world stock exchanges require additional disclosures regarding environmental risks and other externalities. More and more, companies need to think about their fiduciary duty to protect the environment. It can also provide an early warning system for companies who account for these externalities, as Puma saw when they completed their environmental profit and loss report. It has shown them insights into their supply chain, where they need to focus their efforts to reduce carbon emissions and review supplier conduct to find efficiencies and better manage waste.

Puma's method was simple: measure their scope one to four carbon emissions, water and land use, and assign a dollar value for the cost of use. This is something any business can do. Unfortunately, we get a bit hung up on how hard and new it is, and it prevents accountants from implementing this important cost analysis.

Part of the challenge for your business may be understanding which specific environmental impacts to focus on (i.e., how to take everything into account properly and assign a dollar figure). You may be surprised, however, at what resources are out there for your industry already.

Take farming, for example. There is a very real connection between business profits and the environment in a farming business, but almost no farmer takes these things into account. The farmer plants their seeds or plantlets. Rain and good soil quality is needed for them to grow, and the farmer needs to be able to harvest them in order to make money. Otherwise, all the money spent on purchasing the seedlings, fertilising and watering them, caring for them, has been spent in vain. All that potential profit evaporates when an extended rainy season blows through, rotting the plants as they sit in the ground.

Climate change presents extreme risks to the industry, from losses due to storms, droughts, lack of rainfall at the right time, too much rainfall at the wrong time, pest invasions, blights, as well as soil erosion and degradation. Any one of these things can devastate a farmer's crops for the season and wipe out their profits for the year.

Other industries, like manufacturing, find their environmental fiduciary duty in monitoring and managing their waste. They need to ensure they aren't leaking toxins into waterways, contaminating groundwater or polluting the air in the process of making their products. Otherwise, they are fined by local and state governments and will likely face civil, if not criminal, lawsuits. The class action suit, *Anderson, et al. v. Pacific Gas and Electric*, which made Erin Brockovich famous, saw the utility company's first settlement in this case in 1996. It was the largest settlement in U.S. history: $333 million. Pacific Gas then spent the next twenty years and more than $750 million on clean-up efforts. If you add their legal costs and additional $300 million in settlements on top, Pacific Gas has spent over a billion dollars for their toxic waste dumping and I can guarantee you it would not have cost that much to build some concrete-lined pools to contain that toxic water in the first place.

These kinds of court cases and fines to big business are becoming the benchmark for how costly it can be to ignore the environment. It's why local governments spend so much monitoring air, land, and water pollution.

Other companies have knowingly put their employees or customers at risk and were fined millions of dollars. Ford's Pinto safety controversy is an excellent example of prioritising callous accounting over doing no harm to society. The Pinto car had an alarming safety issue where it would burst into flames when rear-ended. In 1973, Ford released a cost-benefit analysis that estimated to recall and modify all 12.5 million cars would cost $137 million, whereas it would only cost $45 million for the 180 burn deaths and 180 serious injuries per year. The irony here is that Ford was then fined and sued, resulting in payouts in excess of the original recall costs.

The lesson here is that the balance sheet is not the only measurement metric.

Key Performance Indicators (KPIs)

Environmental KPIs are often viewed as less important in larger corporations, which can impact their effectiveness. I urge you not to do this, especially when many are directly linked to increases in profit or decreases in costs. Any time there is any perception of competing priorities, the profit-driven one will take precedence in the short-term, even if that will have a negative impact in the long-term. Let's say you have two KPIs: increase profit and reduce carbon footprint, but increasing profit is priority number one. If one of the projects involves spending money to reduce your carbon footprint and save money down the road, that project will never happen because the more important KPI of increasing profit will take precedence. This means your environmental KPI never has the chance to be successful. Staggering the importance of KPIs limits your company to focus only on finances when there are many other factors that affect the day-to-day business operations.

So, how do you measure your environmental impacts and track those numbers? Here is a list of potential indicators you can track in your business:
- Waste reduction from reducing, refusing, and reusing materials
- Office or building energy consumption
- Office employees' gas and oil consumption through work commutes
- Consumption of water
- Overall carbon footprint reduction

Let's examine each of these in this chapter to show how you can apply this to your business today.

One of the great benefits of joining Bullfrog Power and Carbonfund.org is that it creates incentives for your business to lower its energy usage. You pay Bullfrog Power an additional fee each month to supply renewable power to the grid, reducing society's dependence on fossil fuels. If you are offsetting your usage and it's costing your business an extra $400 a year to do so, it increases your motivation to determine where the energy is being wasted. For example, a simple change to LED light bulbs in your building can create big savings. Also, many businesses leave escalators running all weekend long, even if there is no one in the building. Lights are on in office towers, but no one is at the work stations and computer monitors are left on idle. Burning electricity is burning money. But creating an incentive lowers your carbon offsets—suddenly changing behaviour becomes much more likely.

This was evident when a five cent charge was introduced for using plastic bags at checkouts in Toronto, Canada. Reusable shopping bags were introduced in the early 1990s to use instead of free plastic bags that were common in grocery stores across North America. However, these reusable bags cost upwards of $1 each. To the general consumer, as long as there were free bags there was no monetary incentive to switch behaviours, despite the negative impact on the environment. The innovative act of charging five cents per plastic bag caused a significant influx in the use and purchase of reusable bags. A reusable bag can be used for several years and the five cent charge turned it into a money-saving vehicle. If you are a family of four, shopping once per week, buying an average of five bags per trip, that's 5 x 52 x $0.05 = $13.

Not spending $13 on plastic bags each year and instead spending $5 on the same number of canvas bags one time saves you $13 every subsequent year. Suddenly it becomes economical to reuse rather than to continue with the plastic bags. Additionally, the five cent charge created a cultural shift that caused certain demographics to want to carry reusable bags.

In David Suzuki's *Green Guide*, he states that 97% of the Canadian population recycle at least some of the time. By recycling and composting, you can lower your garbage collection bill in communities that charge by the bag.

Every year in the U.S., more than 150 million tons of recyclable products and packaging are processed into raw material for manufacturing.
While we've established that recycling is not the sole answer but is part of the
solution, studies show recycling is clearly more environmentally responsible
than incinerating or dumping waste.

Most Commonly Recycled Products	Positive Environment Impact
Aluminum	Requires only 5% of the energy needed compared to the creation from raw materials.
Appliances (mostly steel)	Reduces mining waste by 97%, virgin material use by 90%, air pollution by 86%, water pollution by 76%, energy use by 74%, and water use by 40%.
One Ton of Paper	Saves 17 trees, 359 litres (79 gallons) of oil, 31,780 litres (7,000 gallons) of water, 2.5 cubic metres (3.3 cubic yards) of landfill space.
One Metre Stack of Newspapers	Saves one tree.
Lead Acid Car	Removes hazardous waste that leaches toxic chemicals into the ground.

Source: David Suzuki's *Green Guide*

Table 2 Recyclable Products and Their Impact

Running a More Cost-effective Office

We've busted the myth that going green is more expensive, but let's look at the actual numbers. Below is a summary of the cost savings from reducing your environmental impact:

Cost Saving Action	How	Cost Savings
Skip bottled water	Avoid providing individual water bottles for employees and move away from a water cooler. Optionally, install a water filter for your tap.	Savings will vary based on your local utility pricing, but typical costs per liter are 100 times cheaper for tap water than bottled. Employees will also not have to spend time replacing the water cooler jug when it's empty.
Be conservative with climate control	If your employees are in sweaters in summer and complaining about the heat in winter, adjust the climate control by a few degrees to flip that dynamic. Reduce usage outside of business hours with a programmable thermostat. Improve efficiency with better insulation or a more efficient boiler.	Depending on your location, climate control can be one of the biggest costs associated with your physical space after rent. Changing usage patterns is free to implement and a programmable thermostat is a small cost for a large impact.
Buy used	Source used or refurbished equipment and furniture to divert from landfills.	Sourcing used equipment or furniture can reduce your costs by about fifty percent. It can take longer to find the right equipment and your office may be an eclectic mix of furniture styles, but that can become an influence in thrifty work culture.

Cost Saving Action	How	Cost Savings
Decrease electronics' energy use	Power off work stations (computers, monitors, and other desktop electronics) outside of business hours. Adjust computer sleep settings to come on within ten to fifteen minutes of being idle.	A computer can use up to 600 kWh a year when left on while not in use. This can save up to $80 per desk annually, which adds up with more employees and overtime.
Update lighting to LEDs	Use LED bulbs when replacing light bulbs.	LED bulbs use ten times less energy than incandescent bulbs and last fifty times as long, saving almost $300 over the lifetime of a single LED bulb. See the calculations later in this chapter.
Conduct an energy audit	Monitoring the usage of your climate control, appliances, and other equipment can help you spot inefficiencies.	Finding the places that use the most energy in your business can help you identify opportunities to decrease energy costs. This can help identify leaks or machinery that needs to be serviced or updated to run more efficiently. Chapter Eleven contains more details on how to conduct an energy audit and its benefits.
Print double-sided	If you must print, make the default to print double-sided.	This can save 25-50% of your paper use.
Skip the printer	If your need to print is minimal, do so at a local print shop instead of having a printer at the office.	Without a printer, you save on purchasing, maintenance, electricity, paper, and ink at the cost of the print shop's fees per page and time to pick up the copies. Check the costs at your local print shop against how often you have to print to determine your savings.

Cost Saving Action	How	Cost Savings
Move paperwork to the cloud	Find a cloud solution that works for your business.	Actual cost savings vary widely based on your business's paper use. You can expect to save a large portion of current paper and ink spending, plus increase productivity as employees don't have to spend time filing and retrieving files. Chapter Fourteen talks in depth about the benefits of moving your data to the cloud.
Travel less	Consider telecommuting when physical presence is not strictly required. Plan trips that are necessary in groupings to reduce overall travel.	While face-to-face meetings are advantageous in certain situations, virtual meetings can satisfy most of the same needs. The cost savings depend on how far and frequently you travel, but can often be cut 25-50% with these guidelines. Savings go beyond just the cost of a plane ticket, where the majority of the carbon emissions are, and include saving on hotels and meals for the traveling employee.
Consider remote working	Allow employees to work from home by investing in online infrastructure.	If you can go fully remote for some job categories, you can eliminate your office space needs entirely. Even having some employees work from home on certain days and share desk space can reduce office requirements such as rent. Remote work is considered a perk and can also help reduce employee turnover by improving work-life balance and saving your employees money in commuting costs.
Reduce waste	Complete a waste audit to understand where your waste is coming from and take steps to reduce this waste.	Waste costs are often hidden, but can be reduced through waste diversion and avoidance. Chapter Eleven contains more details on how to conduct a waste audit and its benefits.

Source: *Greening Your Office* by Jill Doucette and Lee Johnson

Table 3 Cost savings potentials in your office

Energy

One of the easiest changes to make is switching from incandescent lights to compact fluorescent lamps (CFL) or LED. From David Suzuki's *Green Guide*, the cost breakdown is as follows:

Operating Details	Incandescent	CFL	LED
Typical bulb cost	0.40	2.60	3.00
Average life in hours	1,000	10,000	50,000
Average cost of electricity ($/kwh)	0.10	0.10	0.10
Power use in kWh	0.06	0.015	0.005
Cost to operate for 50,000 hours	$300	$75	$25
Life cycle cost (purchase price plus electricity)	$320	$88	$28
Cost per hour of use	$0.0064	$0.00176	$0.00056
TOTAL SAVINGS		$232	$292

Table 4 Comparing Light Bulb Life Cycle Costs

While the total savings is higher with CFL bulbs, LED lights have a lower cost per use, which is an important calculation when comparing a more expensive but longer lasting item to a cheaper alternative.

Based on David Suzuki's *Green Guide*, using LED in traffic lights saved

Vancouver $350,000 annually. Work crews only have to replace them every few years, and they reduce energy use by up to 90%, which saved the city on both maintenance and electricity costs.

MAJOR USES OF ENERGY IN HOMES

Home Energy Use	Australia	Canada	UK	US
Space heating/cooling	39%	57%	60%	49%
Appliances and electronics	29%	13%	14%	20%
Water heating	27%	24%	23%	15%
Lighting	5%	5%	3%	7%

Source: David Suzuki's *Green Guide*

Table 5 Energy Use By Country

In every country, the majority of home energy use is from heating and cooling. Identify holes where air is escaping and costing you money—plugging these leaks can reduce costs by up to 30%. On an average energy bill of $120, this could result in savings as high as $36. Weather stripping and caulking around windows and doors are a great investment, saving an average of $1.54 per dollar invested. That's an average of 54% ROI on your home improvements, which are a tax write-off! It is a small, yet powerful, way to save money and go green.

Appliances and electronics are the second highest percentage for energy use in the home, according to Suzuki. Looking back to Chapter Six, you can see how much of an impact a green power bar can have on your costs. Energy leaking can cost homes and businesses an extra 75% on energy costs.

Energy Efficiency

An easy way to identify energy leaks is by reviewing your overnight or downtime consumption. I'm going to assume your business doesn't work around the clock, so there should be a time period when energy usage should be approaching nil. If there is still significant usage at this time, investigate the cause as this will reduce your baseline energy consumption. It is usually the most effective change to implement.

Plot a year's worth of energy data to compare each month's energy consumption against the previous twelve months to highlight any upward or downward trends. This will show any seasonal trends that you can measure against other buildings in your area. This is especially important in Canada and other cold climates, where heating in winter and cooling in summer shift your energy consumption. You should pay particular attention to whether the heating costs drop during the spring. If they don't, your heating is not being adequately adjusted for the warmer weather and your staff are probably compensating by opening windows and wasting energy. Ventilating in this manner is extremely costly and inefficient. Talk with your building manager every spring to ensure they monitor and alter the thermostat if you are not able to alter it yourself.

You can also use degree days to make a more robust check on space heating requirements. The number of degree days in a month is a measure of the severity of cold weather. Check out Carbon Trust (carbontrust.com) for a description of how to use them.

If your business or home office has air conditioning as well as heating, then you're likely to have double the carbon footprint of those without. Therefore, it is important to ensure your offices are as energy efficient as possible to minimize costs. Some tips to help you to do that:

- Run a 'Switch it off' campaign. Label light switches with "Please turn off when not in use" and email your staff to request them to turn off lights in unused areas. Dispel myths that it's more efficient to leave lights on than to continually switch them on and off. This isn't true, especially with LED lights and other modern light bulbs.

- Ensure all computers and monitors are plugged into TrickleStar PowerStrips to prevent baseload drain. When laptops, phones, and whatnot are charged to full power, but still plugged in, they continue to draw power from the outlet, which wastes energy and money. Unplug laptops to save the charge in your home office.
- Remind employees to turn off their computers at night. Post a sign on the door to remind them, when they are leaving, to turn off all lights and switch off their computer.
- Provide energy consumption information to your staff so they are aware of how much money and energy is being wasted.
- Set heating and cooling to 17°C (68°F) and 25°C (77°F), respectively. Energy consumption is tripled when your air conditioner is set to 24°C and it takes ten times more money and electricity to cool your office by 3°C more when it's set to 20°C. If your staff are wearing scarves and cardigans to work, you need to raise your air conditioning temperatures.
- At night, make sure to turn down the heat during the winter and turn off the air conditioning during the summer. During winter, the temperature of an office can be brought down to 14°C (58°F), which will still keep the pipes from freezing but is not wasting energy by unnecessarily heating an empty office.
- Encourage staff to only boil as much water as necessary in the kettle. It takes ten times the energy to boil double the water, so it is an incredibly wasteful and expensive exercise to continually boil water that will not be used.
- Ensure that any air conditioning unit is being ventilated properly. If the hot exhaust air is not being properly ventilated away from the unit, it will be trying to suck up its own hot exhaust, which is inefficient.
- Similarly, clean the air conditioning unit regularly. The filter needs to be cleaned once every six months to ensure maximum functionality. The best part of regularly maintaining the unit is that it will last longer and save you even more money down the road by extending its life and by not having to pay a special waste fee.

- Install curtains or shades on all windows for summertime to prevent unnecessary overheating of your office, which will in turn reduce your energy bill and save you money.
- Ensure all hot water pipes are properly insulated. Otherwise, the cost of the heating loss is like throwing dollar bills out the window.

If you find the above to be excessive, consider implementing one step to start. Depending on where you live and seasonal variations in climate, some of the above tips may not be relevant or will need to be tweaked to best suit your lifestyle. If you work at night, for example, because most of your business is with partners who are overseas, it may be more prudent to investigate heat and cooling losses first to maximize your appliances before altering temperatures to best suit your comfort.

GENERAL KNOWLEDGE TIP: Note that electricity and energy are not the same thing. Electricity can be created by using different forms of energy (gas and oil mains, compressed air) that all have a different carbon footprint.

PRO TIP: If you run your business out of your home office, rather than heating the entire house all day while you're home alone, consider leaving the rest of the house at a lower temperature and shutting the door to your office so a space heater can heat that space. Even better, forgo the space heater entirely and bundle up by putting on a sweater.

Digital Thermostats

Digital thermostats are a way to increase your comfort in your own home while saving energy. You can set them on a schedule based on your life as most are connected to apps controlled from your phone. This allows for you to not waste energy when you're away from home or are sleeping but with enough flexibility that you can still turn your air conditioning on early if your schedule suddenly changes.

Water

A running tap uses approximately eight litres, or two gallons, of water per minute. This cost breaks down to approximately a dollar per minute. While a dollar doesn't seem like that much, think about running the tap when you brush your teeth. You brush twice a day and let the tap run for one minute per brushing session. This adds up to $730 in water costs per year for just you. Imagine if your whole household stopped this wasteful behaviour. If you could save this much money with one small action, there will be other ways your business and home are using water that could be more efficient and less wasteful. Consider doing a water audit by writing a diary for a week of times you used water and for how long you ran the tap. Check your usage against your water bill and see if your math is close to how much your water metre is measuring. If it is not, you may have a leak or need to re-evaluate how you are utilising your water.

Tips:

- Turn off the tap while brushing teeth, washing dishes, and shaving
- Use a bucket and sponge to wash your car
- Sweep your driveway instead of using a hose
- Keep a jug of water in the fridge for cold water
- Wash fruits and vegetables in a basin
- Reuse water, like the fruits and vegetable basin water, for plants or other projects

Another area to save money is the water infrastructure of your home or business. Leaks can waste significant amounts of water and are a hidden cost. To detect leaks, read your water meter before and after a two-hour period when no water is used. If the meter reading isn't exactly the same at both times, you have a leak. Check the toilet for leaks by adding food colouring to the tank and waiting 15 minutes. If you notice any colouring in the toilet bowl, there is a leak. Most replacement parts are inexpensive, readily available and easy to install. Toiletology (toiletology.com) is an exceptional resource to improve your toilet efficiency.

Lunch and Learn

In the hierarchy of environmental lunches, purchasing lunch is usually the hardest on our planet and packed lunches from home aren't always much better. However, bringing home-cooked meals to the office can be done in an environmentally-friendly and cost-saving way. See the table on page 89 for more details.

Going Even Greener: Greening Your Supply Chain

An easy way to reduce your company's environmental footprint is to make it company policy to buy environmentally-friendly products and services. This avoids any potential issues for your company, like accidentally purchasing hazardous materials, and it strengthens the market for environmentally and socially responsible goods.

An important aspect of greening your supply chain is considering the amount of product you buy. Over-purchasing products, especially those with a limited shelf life, isn't an efficient use of your space or your dollar. This is a good example of hidden costs. Buying material to simply throw it away is bad business.

Questions to ask when ordering new supplies:
- Do we need it?
- Can we do with less?
- Can we buy it in quantities that better match our needs?
- Will we use it within its shelf life?
- Where is it made?
- Does it support jobs, businesses, and the tax base in your local area or country?
- Does the production create unnecessary pollution?

LUNCH STUDY

SAVE YOUR FAMILY $450 A YEAR
USING ECO-FRIENDLY REUSABLE LUNCHWARE

Lunch Items	Daily Cost	Annual Cost*	Daily Disposable Lunch Trash	Yearly Disposable Lunch Trash	Yearly Savings† By Going Waste-free
Plastic Sandwich Baggy	$0.06 per unit	$32.40	3 pieces	540 pieces	
Reusable Food Container	0	0	0	0	$32.40 SAVINGS
Paper Napkin	$0.02	$10.80	3	540	
Reusable Napkin	0	0	0	0	$10.80 SAVINGS
Plastic Spoon	$0.04	$21.60	3	540	
Reusable Utensil	0	0	0	0	$21.60 SAVINGS
Juice box	$0.44 per serving	$237.60	3	540	
Juice in Reusable Bottle	$0.27	$145.80	0	0	$91.80 SAVINGS
Pre-packaged Yogurt	$0.95	$513.00	3	540	
Yogurt in Resuable Tin	$0.60	$324.00	0	0	$189.00 SAVINGS
Pre-packaged Snack Mix	$0.45	$243.00	3	540	
Snack Mix in Reusable Tin	$0.30	$162.00	0	0	$108.00 SAVINGS

ELIMINATE THOUSANDS OF
PIECES OF TRASH
USING REUSABLE LUNCHWARE

18 Pieces of Trash per family Every Day

3,240 Pieces of Trash per family Every Year

$453⁶⁰ Savings per family Every Year

* Annual is calculated at 180 days of packed lunches. This is the average length of a school year in the U.S. Family is calculated as 2 kids and 1 adult.
† Cost savings is achieved by purchasing food in family-size packages and packing lunch in reusable containers instead of using throw-away and buying more expensive pre-packaged, single-serving juice, yogurt, and dry snacks.

Data and Table Based on information from ECOlunchbox

Figure 2 Financial Savings for Reuse Compared to Disposables

- Is it recyclable? Is it made of recycled materials?
- What impact does this have on your people?
- What will these supplies or equipment cost to operate—in both money and energy—over their lifetime?
- What wastes are created by your purchasing decisions? How will you dispose of them?

Environmentally Preferable Purchasing

Every purchase your company makes is a vote. Every time you buy something, you're voting for that type of product, service, or business. When you spend money, what questions are you asking suppliers about where the products originated and what will happen after your business is finished with them? Incorporate these questions into your purchasing decisions to support other products and services that reduce harm to the environment and workers. In their book, *Greening Your Office*, Jill Doucette and Lee Johnson have numerous examples that you can take into consideration. Here are a few things you can do:

- Be clear what's important to your business, your customers, and their customers.
- Review environmental purchasing policies of other companies, such as Unilever, to get ideas.
- Select your key environmental criteria and review your company's supply room to check your inventory against these environmental criteria.
  - Use environmental scorecards like Green Story (greenstory.ca).
- After you identify items that should be replaced, see if your suppliers have alternatives available to meet your requirements or if they can develop them.
- Use life cycle thinking, especially for large purchases. For example, when you buy a printer, you can consider its energy efficiency, ink yields, duplexing capacity, and both cartridge and end-of-life recycling options.
- Don't buy things you don't need or too much of what you do need, and don't buy goods that come with packaging that will cost money to dispose.

- Collaborate. Ask other businesses how they save money by reducing waste. Share tips that you discover and ask your networks to share theirs. You may be surprised by the ideas and solutions this sparks.

Green scorecards are a way to apply best practices into everyday decisions. It clearly outlines company priorities and allows employees to execute decisions within these mandates. Plus, it can save you money. For example, if being energy efficient is a priority, it needs to be reflected in purchasing, acquiring items that save energy and, inevitably, saving money.

Back to your dollar as a vote, if suppliers know their clients are looking for environmental products, it increases their motivation to go green.

Clearing the Rising Sustainability Bar

Humanity is advancing all the time. We are constantly discovering new ways our products are damaging to the environment or other vulnerable populations. When this becomes known to the public or policy makers, there tends to be a push to pass regulation to prevent this harm from continuing. Sometimes this could mean a legal case ruling against a company or professional certifications adjusting their standards. Or it could be the government passing an emission tax, like they have in London. In the B Corp certification, for example, every two years they strive to improve their assessment and encourage companies to continue to also improve if they wish to remain certified.

Small businesses are at a distinct advantage in this regard because they are adaptive and able to change with market trends, allowing them to more accurately and more often hit a moving target. Staying above the rising bar makes good business sense, and not only because it can be profitable. If you're constantly reacting, you risk losing market share to innovators while you're spending time adjusting resources. Three main drivers to be environmental:

- Consumers are demanding better environmental performance
- Governments are looking for ways to limit environmental damage and to guide investment toward the environmental and economic benefits of the new energy economy

- Businesses are looking to reduce risk and build profits, and for greener suppliers to support greener products and operations

Underlying all these is that we are coming to terms with the inescapable environmental realities that underlie our economic well-being. We need to stay above the rising bar, guiding our actions with a cradle-to-cradle approach, and doing the right thing the first time, because it's good business. You don't want your business to be dragged, kicking and screaming, into that future. You want to lead the way.

To stay above the rising bar, create an environmental purchase policy to decrease the amount of time required to purchase products. Typical policies are comprised of waste minimization, recycled content, energy efficiency, pollution, preferred suppliers, and questions to ask future and current suppliers.

While business as usual doesn't include social and environmental responsibility as a part of our business structure, these days it's important for businesses to make incremental changes to keep up with the ever-increasing costs of not doing so.

Nine

Collaborating with Stakeholders

No business is an island. There are many people and entities that encounter your business throughout its lifetime. Some may be present at the beginning or during periods of rapid growth, like a bank or investors, and then absent for long periods of time. Others are a constant and are essential to its livelihood, like employees and suppliers.

As shown with the Beekeeper's Naturals, stakeholders to your business are an important consideration, as they all impact your business profits in different ways. Some stakeholders influence profit directly through cost, whereas others are potential threats, such as competitors homing in on your market share.

Here is a list of external stakeholders:
- Employees
- Suppliers
- Consumers
- Governments and Regulatory Agencies
- Competitors
- Shareholders and Investors
- Banks and Lenders
- Trade unions
- Owners
- General public

All of these business stakeholders have their own goals and motivations, as well as potential costs and benefits. Some can be competing, as competitors are traditionally seen as dangerous to the existence of your business if they have an advantage that could cut into your market share.

Let's break down some of these stakeholders, how they can impact your finances, and ways you can work with them for win-win scenarios on all sides.

Employees

Lack of productivity, mistrust, high turnover. Losing an employee costs up to five times their salary to replace them. If you treat your employees well, they will be more committed and willing to go above and beyond. Google and other startups know this, as they consistently find ways to make their employees happy and have become mega-giants in the process. Gourmet lunches, pet-friendly offices, work-life balance, entertainment—it's working in luxury.

My own work history has a tell-tale example of treating employees respectfully. I worked for a company who were appreciative of my work and gave me time in lieu for time above my 40-hour work week, at least for the first year. Unfortunately, this abruptly changed. I was pulled into the boss's office to be told I hadn't been keeping my hours properly and, ostensively, passively accused of stealing hours from the company. This then triggered a performance review that took me by surprise. Meanwhile, it had been a miscommunication of company processes that was taken in bad faith. I was furious. And I immediately stopped doing extra overtime. My productivity plummeted. I also ended up leaving, which, as noted above, was then costly for the company to replace me.

High turnover in small businesses is far more noticeable than in a larger company that has standard training and recruitment processes. Wages are the largest cost for a small business and can be an easy area to save money. Treating your workers fairly and approaching mistakes with a forgiving attitude will go a long way to making your employees feel welcome and safe at work.

The CEO must understand this on a fundamental level because it is a top-down cost. If you can't manage your people well and help them feel appreciated, it will contribute to a costly revolving door of employees coupled with expensive training.

Team morale is an environmental issue. Without engaged employees, there is no incentive for them not to fall back into business as usual. Also, by engaging your employees you create an environment that is making changes and preventing expensive turnover costs. This is especially important in an age where every business wants to attract top talent. Two tech companies based in Toronto—Fiix and Open Concept—compete with tech giants for talent. Their competitive edge is in their mission, as both of them are B Corp certified and attract millennial employees. They also found that after a year and a half of minimizing environmental impact and doing more for the community, staff were staying and highly-educated people were applying to work there because of their ethical and environmental values. Seventy percent of people believe that being green is good for business, and that we should incorporate those practices into our businesses. This turns you into a magnet that attracts and keeps the best talent.

Employees who are encouraged to take action in the workplace and share their ideas to make the company better for the planet feel empowered and become more loyal to the company. Many studies link higher employee satisfaction to those working for green companies because they feel the company is held to a higher level of integrity. It also offers opportunities for team building. Successful campaigns for going green include bringing employees into decision-making positions, which builds valuable teamwork and team-building skills. Engaging employees in decision-making processes helps offices gain momentum and support as a result of the ideas generated internally from a variety of employees, not just a few 'green-keeners'. Going green can give staff something to be proud of in their day-to-day activities, while also meeting your organizational goals of being an ethical entrepreneur.

Continued Success: Beau's Brewery

We are currently in a transitionary period where businesses large and small are converting to sustainable practices to ward off atrophy. Businesses like

Patagonia, Chipotle Mexican Grill, and Unilever are invigorating their businesses with environmental practices. And others, like Amazon and Walmart, are falling into the vicious cycle of unhappy employees leaving, costing the company money, which means less to invest in employees. Potential opportunities for growth or revenue generation are missed because the company is in a constant state of hiring and training staff. This is a compounding issue, where the costs and risks are all interlinked.

Once trust has been lost with employees, trade partners or other stakeholders, it's difficult to rebuild the relationship without it coming across as pandering. All too often, it is an ongoing issue with bad customer service or mismanagement of supply chains that leads to this vicious cycle.

On the other hand, when a business builds a foundation of purpose and sustainability, they are able to bring all stakeholders together in support of their business. One such business is Beau's Brewery. Beau's founded their company on sustainability, which has been a huge advantage to their productivity, talent retention, and, inevitably, has provided huge savings on otherwise hidden costs.

Beau's developed a positive work culture by implementing the following:

- Provided an employee ownership program, where employees can buy equity in the company.
- While quickly growing their company, they utilized their B Corp certification to attract a certain type of employee.
- Hired a culture ambassador to facilitate organic growth of a positive culture.
- Hired entry-level positions from the immediate area with the intent to cultivate specialized skills.
- Allowed telecommuting whenever possible to provide flexibility.
- Provided an office in Ottawa, a nearby city, to reduce commuting all the way to the brewery. It decreased environmental impact (gas consumption) and increased employee quality of life.
- Implemented an anonymous employee feedback system in order to monitor employee happiness and engagement, so they can address issues

as they arise. This is especially important for folks who cannot bring these issues to their direct manager.

- Their CEO is committed to doing the right moral thing, even if it is not immediately profitable, because it confirms their company's mission in a tangible way.

Located in a small town, Beau's could have faced the significant challenge of finding appropriate highly-skilled people. Because their culture resonated with a specific demographic, they attracted a diverse group willing to come to them. For example, they hired a QA lab manager from Africa who relocated to work with them. Beau's created a product and culture that turned them into a magnet.

When a company stands for something more than making widgets, it engages people in unexpected ways. The CFO has said, "We'll cut something somewhere else to stay sustainable and green," keeping that at the forefront of the culture. One of her initiatives was the Greener Futures Project, a members-only beer club that received exclusive beers, and used 100% of the revenue (yes, revenue, not profit) to fund green initiatives. The first thing they paid for was a Bullfrog Power partnership, allowing Beau's to use green electricity and natural gas. This is a fascinating and innovative business model where they are transparent, allowing their clients to contribute through product purchasing and know the impact of their purchase.

Shareholders and Investors

The reason a shareholder invests in your company is complex. There is a growing market of consumers dedicated to sustainability and eco-friendly business practices. Now, more than ever, there is a high cost of inaction and a missed revenue opportunity. In the white paper, "Scaling Up Sustainable Procurement", the average length of implementation of sustainable projects was seven or more years. Companies who jumped into sustainability in 2013 are now seeing multi-faceted benefits. If your company isn't doing the same already, shareholders and investors will be asking why.

Outside of direct benefits to the environment, being the first adopter in your industry of sustainable policy is advantageous on a few fronts. To start, it places you in a leadership role where you create industry standards. Imagine being the influencer to establish standard practices, to provide guides on what works and what doesn't, as well as being acknowledged as the innovator that you know you are. And think of how this would impact your image with shareholders.

But also, it's inevitable that environmental regulations will be put in place going forward. Being ahead of the curve on environmental regulations allows you to budget for change, before your shareholders are threatening to divest their shares or demand your resignation. Most decisions in favour of the environment will be cost-effective in the long-term, but do have start-up expenditures. Making changes on your own timeline, instead of being given dates for regulation compliance, is easier on your budget and allows for more organic and thoughtful changes.

All of this connects to shareholders because they invest in companies with strong financials and are now looking for positive environmental policies as well. It could be the difference that makes you stand out in the crowd. As you grow, your company may need outside investors who can inject much-needed cash into your business. These investors may be people you know or are related to, or they could be complete strangers. Your long-term business success will be paramount to these investors; if your business fails, they lose their investment. Of course, if things take off, they will be rewarded. However, it is why they are an important stakeholder to consider, as investors can help scale up your business.

Larry Fink, CEO of global investment managing company BlackRock Investment Stewardship, has written extensively about BlackRock's approach to include environmental, social, and governance (ESG) screens as part of their investment strategies. In previous years, Fink specifically mentioned that a company's social, environmental, or governance policies often signal operational excellence. BlackRock has made their own ESG integrations and expects their investing companies to have done the same. It also indicates if a company is overly concerned with short-term profit, which can be detrimental to an investor's long-term goal of saving for retirement or simply a stable investment market.

Suppliers

Let's go back to Arthur Andersen LLP, Enron's accounting firm, for a moment. In the Enron scandal, Arthur Andersen LLP was dragged down in the turmoil. Now, they were guilty of numerous offences, but had Enron been ethical, could Arthur Andersen LLP have committed crimes? If Arthur Andersen LLP had stood by their accounting scruples, could the whole economic crash have been prevented? The alliance between the client, Enron, and the supplier, Arthur Andersen LLP, was based on unethical practices. Too big to fail? Absolutely not. This can be contrasted by Beekeeper's Naturals saving their business by using only pure raw product.

Suppliers can have the power to make or break your business. Sony learned this the hard way during Christmas season in 2001. Nearly 1.3 million PlayStation game consoles were stopped at the Dutch border because they contained too much of a toxic element, cadmium, in the units. At the time, their supplier in China had manufactured the goods but had not taken into account this potential violation of European regulations. Sony then bore the cost of replacing the parts that had excess cadmium. Not to mention the millions of dollars in lost revenue, as PlayStation was a best-selling product at the time, Christmas is when game consoles have their peak sales volume for the year. The following year, Sony implemented a 'Green Partner Environmental Quality Approval Program' policy, where Sony would only partner with suppliers who met strict environmental regulations in places like Europe, so such an event would never happen again.

As more and more companies follow suit with sustainable purchasing policies, it becomes an integral part of supplier relations. In the same sustainable procurement white paper mentioned earlier, research of surveyed companies showed that in 2013, these focuses were critically important for cost saving and risk reduction. In contrast, in 2017 the same companies were implementing these policies for the benefits of value generation and branding instead. This shift illustrates the learning that has come out of implementing and analyzing the effects of these policies in the long term. Sustainable purchasing policies not only benefit the company by saving money but also play a more active role in profit generation and brand value.

HOW IMPORTANT ARE THE FOLLOWING PRIORITIES FOR YOUR PROCUREMENT/ SUPPLY CHAIN ORGANIZATION?

Main priorities of procurement organizations 2013 vs 2017

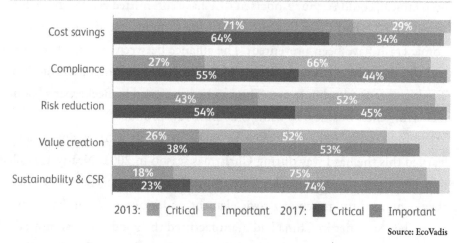

Source: EcoVadis

Figure 3 Procurement organization priorities, 2013 vs 2017

Consumers

Consumers are a critical stakeholder in your business. Without them, you are nothing. Therefore, it is important to cater and listen to consumer concerns and adapt your business accordingly. As I have mentioned in previous chapters, there is a growing market of consumers wanting to be mindful of the environment in their purchases. In the same white paper, 90% of the industry leaders implementing sustainable purchasing policies saw a 33% increase in revenue over competitors, due to growing customer demand for sustainably-sourced products. The old phrase 'the customer is king' rings true when we consider going green. You know your consumers best and how they influence your business.

As said before, the competitive advantage of early adoption allows you more time for trial and error but also lets you customize your product to the specific feedback of your consumers. And they will let you know when you succeed, either by their dollars or by reviews. Marketing your sustainable practices leads to greater brand recognition and loyalty, as consumers know that you are the go-to brand for sustainable product or service choices.

Government

Government provides the infrastructure on which businesses rely. From currency to roads and from subsidies to regulations, the government is in fact a stakeholder that wants you to succeed. When business booms, the economy booms and that is a wonderful thing. However, the government is usually seen as a barrier to success with regulations, laws, taxes, and fines. The cost of not complying can be astronomical, but the intent is to provide safety for consumers and businesses alike.

Here are some government initiatives that can benefit you as a business person and a consumer:

- **Tax breaks and incentives:** Governments will often provide tax breaks or incentives to help lower your tax bill in a particular year, in order to keep more money in your business, so you can invest more in growing your company.
- **Grants to minimize risk:** Governments understand that small businesses are the lifeblood of a nation's economy and will often provide grant money to businesses that fit a certain criteria. Usually these criteria are chosen from national survey data and are intended to help new businesses or businesses in sectors facing some economic challenges.
- **Subsidies:** Governments give big businesses millions of dollars in subsidies each year. Usually, the intent of subsidies is to offset the cost of sustainable initiatives, either for installing solar panels or replacing your machinery to be more energy efficient.

- **Infrastructure:** Local, provincial or state, and federal governments are responsible for building and maintaining roads, public transport, collecting garbage, providing the electricity, water, and heat that you have access to, and helps your business succeed.

Elizabeth Warren, a U.S. Senator, has a favourite quote that I love and think is important to remember when considering the role of support governments have to businesses:

There is nobody in this country who got rich on their own. Nobody. You built a factory out there–good for you. But I want to be clear. You moved your goods to market on roads the rest of us paid for. You hired workers the rest of us paid to educate. You were safe in your factory because of police forces and fire forces that the rest of us paid for. You didn't have to worry that marauding bands would come and seize everything at your factory. Now look. You built a factory and it turned into something terrific or a great idea–God bless! Keep a hunk of it. But part of the underlying social contract is you take a hunk of that and pay forward for the next kid who comes along.

Businesses often have an adversarial attitude or negative opinions of government, but they are an important stakeholder in your business. They can be quite beneficial and helpful as well, especially if you or your employees drive to work. You might find they are receptive to help if you approach them with your concerns with a collaborative and patient attitude.

Taking another look at the EcoVadis study mentioned earlier, there is a striking increase reported in the criticality of sustainable sourcing practices in terms of compliance. While the overall importance of compliance hasn't increased much, the issues have become more urgent as governments enact regulations requiring adherence to sustainable practices. By becoming an early adopter, your business can decrease the cost of compliance by spreading it out over time and taking on the changes in manageable steps rather than rushing to overhaul entire processes at once to comply with new regulations.

Competitors

Similar to the shareholder section, your business needs to stand out in a sea of competitors. You must do things better, faster, and more efficiently or risk eroding profits. Predicting the future regarding the consumer, government regulations, and market is critical to long-term success. And this involves planning. Waste removal, efficient use of energy, timely changes—all of this impacts your bottom line, but also your reputation. Both elements are imperative to blowing your competitors out of the water.

My estimate is that mitigating these risks and costs can increase your profit by at least 20%. Larger businesses can increase their profits by more than 30%, according to Bob Willard's research, so scaling that down to the size of your business means a 20% savings is a reasonable assumption. Incorporating ethical business decisions into every facet of your business will increase your profits. But probably not if you only do it for profitability reasons, as you are likely to miss critical steps along the way. Integrating ethical practices needs to be ingrained and fundamentally fused into all parts of the business to ensure actual profit increase.

It is rare for external stakeholders to be a focus of building a business, but now more than ever there is a critical need to collaborate with these partners. Working with your suppliers or purchasers to find ways to ease pain points not only strengthens your business, but you'll develop a reputation that is powerful in an age where cancel culture can destroy a business overnight.

Ten

Efficiency and the True Cost of Waste

You know reducing waste is more than just a trend and is considered great business sense when ExxonMobil CEO, Darren Woods, advocates for it:

> *Greater energy efficiency is also essential. It might seem counterintuitive, but a big part of ExxonMobil's business is developing products and technologies that help save energy. Examples include our advanced automotive materials that make cars lighter and more fuel-efficient, and improved plastic packaging that reduces the energy needed to ship goods around the world.*

If companies like ExxonMobil are looking to developing efficiencies, why aren't you?

Going Further with Less

Businesses founded on sustainability objectives have become a multi-billion-dollar industry, forging the way in the sustainable economy. Companies leading the way have been studied at length in the book *Green Giants* by Freya Williams and include Chipotle Mexican Grill, Unilever, Whole Foods Market, Natura & Co, and Tesla. Many other companies have product lines that are classified as sustainable—Toyota's Prius, for example—but those principles have not been adopted company-wide. In her book, Williams discusses six key factors that contribute to their international, billion-dollar success. These are:

- The Iconoclastic Leader (the one who started it all)
- Disruptive Innovation
- A Higher Purpose than Profit
- Sustainability as Core Business
- Mainstream Appeal
- Brands Built on Transparency, Responsibility, Collaboration

Many small businesses are founded on more than one of these principles, so adopting the other principles is an achievable goal. Mainstream appeal and building a company that thrives on transparency, responsibility, and collaboration are the two pieces that are most difficult, because they are so often against the grain of the traditional business world.

It can be uncomfortable, for example, to make your company's financials available to the public. Collaboration amongst businesses is still uncommon, because it seems so counterintuitive to business practices taught and reiterated today. The myth that business must closely guard trade secrets has been perpetuated throughout the world to bolster up our current unstable, unsustainable economy. In fact, companies that share their creations in open source platforms often see an increase in sales, because clients who try their software see the value of it and the expertise involved in creating it.

Tobias Utz Mueller-Glodde from CoPower Green Bonds put it best, as he witnessed the success of his father's collaborative workshops using the nucleus approach. To come to these ten person collaborative workshops, a business owner would share one business secret with the rest of the group that had helped them improve their business. The worry from attendees was that they were giving up their secret and would risk losing their competitive advantage, but they didn't realize they would gain nine secrets in exchange for theirs. And even if participants worked in similar areas of town or industries, the exchange of business successes as shared learning is key to growing an industry. It creates an opportunity to increase the size of the pie as a whole for market participants in 'coopertition' (or cooperative competition), while diminishing the perceivedly required notion of zero-sum competition.

Another example where collaboration could help businesses is personal. My brother runs a farm in rural Australia that primarily produces sugar cane. Each September, he harvests the cane and brings it to a mill approximately 80 km south in the neighbouring town. The truck drives to the town full and then has the inefficient trip of returning home empty. At $260 per round trip, making an average of 220 trips during a harvest season, you can see that this is an opportunity.

This cost could be mitigated if he could bring products *back* in his empty vehicle. The by-product of sugar cane is used by farmers as a compostable fertilizer that is not just environmentally-friendly but also Great Barrier Reef friendly, a huge consideration in Queensland. The company responsible for distributing the mill's compostable fertilizer refuses to allow anyone but their people to transport it, even though the farmers supplying that mill are clients. Instead of saving transportation costs all around, my brother and the fertilizer company both have an empty truck on the road 50% of the time. Each company has an added expense, both fiscally and environmentally.

So, let's break it down:

FARMER'S EMPTY TRANSPORT EXPENSE

Expense	Amount
Fuel	$100
Wages	$60
Wear and Tear	$100
Total Expense Per Trip	$260
Total Annual Expense (220 trips per year)	$57,200

Table 6 Farmer Costs

MILL'S EMPTY TRANSPORT EXPENSE

Expense	Amount
Fuel	$90
Wages	$60
Wear and Tear	$70
Total Expense Per Trip	$220
Total Annual Expense (220 trips per year)	$48,400

Table 7 Mill's Costs

Notice the trend here? Both companies are losing money and collaboration could easily correct this problem. As a small business owner, can you imagine having an additional $50,000 in savings for one year? Wasted trips are a huge cost to business, which is why Walmart and Nike have committed to solving this kind of inefficiency in their businesses, by working together with suppliers for an outcome that benefits everyone.

You can incorporate this kind of thinking into your business as well. Here are a few examples:

- If you purchase from the same wholesaler as other local businesses, partner up so only one trip is made for your neighbourhood stores, rather than individual trips for each store
- Similarly, if your business receives deliveries from the same suppliers, consider asking your neighbours if they want to add to your order to minimize the trips your suppliers make
- Collaborate on local advertising, using both sides of a promotion card or flyer to promote two different businesses
- Consider lending or borrowing tools as needed, rather than each store needing to buy their own set
- Ask your suppliers if they will accept returned packaging, boxes or pal-

lets for them to reuse, so they can decrease their costs of buying more and your garbage collection costs decrease

- Encourage your employees to car-share with other folks in the area, to decrease the number of cars on the road

The True Cost of Waste

The cost of waste to a business has been estimated to be between five and 20 times its disposal cost. When you break down everything involved in creation and disposal, it makes a lot more sense. These are a few of the wastes involved in production that are probably costing you money:

- Raw material such as scrap wood from furniture or paper production.
- Auxiliary materials such as plastic wrapping on pallets that is immediately discarded upon delivery, or the helium used in medical equipment that, if not recaptured, is lost forever as it escapes our atmosphere.
- Labour waste includes mostly intangible productivity losses due to inefficient processes or the cleanup involved due to wastage in other areas. This could look like transport drivers waiting for products to be loaded, or office workers managing physical paperwork.
- Energy for excess lighting used due to lack of natural light or using unnecessary extra energy because your machines have not been serviced and, therefore, are not running in an energy efficient way.
- Opportunity cost of not selling wasted product because if you are storing and displaying a product that ends up in the landfill, you could have been selling other products that could have been sold and made you money.
- Disposal such as the additional equipment and materials required to remove waste or the chemicals used to neutralize hazardous waste.
- Recycling, which uses energy and usually only creates lower quality goods. Most recyclable waste doesn't make it to a recycling centre and is therefore wasted.

The true cost of waste tends to increase as you move from goods in to goods out. There is a consistent issue in manufacturing where inefficient assembly lines waste raw product or packing machines spew finished products across the floor, destroying them and their retail value. In these cases, the production manager isn't concerned that the company's profit was being lost right after all that effort went into creating it.

Managing waste: In managing your waste, there is often a hierarchy for determining the eco-efficiency of your organization. Waste hierarchy sets out waste management options in order of preference and focuses on top priorities to implement and adopt, which are frequently the low hanging fruit. These are the easiest options that have the highest impact for waste diversion.

1. Avoid
2. Reduce
3. Reuse
4. Recycle

We all know the saying 'reduce, reuse, recycle' but there hasn't been much focus on avoiding products, and potentially waste, as well as the order of the words. The three Rs are placed in order of what is best for the environment. Notice that recycle is the very last step?

To reduce your waste, follow these steps:

- Analyze your processes and figure out where waste is created.
- What is the allotment going towards waste compared to what you are producing?
- Compare the amount of waste you create to the waste disposal that is being provided and paid for.
- Where are corners being cut that increase waste?
- Where can you prioritize waste reduction and save money?
- What is the systemic reason that causes waste in each situation?
- Establish processes that resolve why waste occurs.

Avoid

We've previously talked about avoiding purchases. (Remember the cute $10 sunglasses?) This is an easy way to decrease costs, clutter, and impact. Consider what your business would look like functioning with the bare minimum, or first trying to source second-hand or refurbished goods before purchasing new ones. Do you need eight different types of pens in three different colours? Do you need a new-fangled gadget? If you see a sale and feel compelled to buy because you're "saving money," this would be a good time to ask someone else in your office if you really need that thing on sale, or if it's going to end up as clutter in a corner somewhere, or if you'll spend more money again to have it taken to landfill, a further waste of money. When you start weighing need versus want, the value of items comes to light.

Reduce

Typically, reduction is done by buying less volume. Another sneaky trick is to look at the versatility of a purchase. Vinegar can be a cleaner, a condiment, a laundry soap, a skin treatment—the list goes on. Purchasing items with multiple functions is an environmental trick and significantly reduces impact. Rather than buying sixteen different cleaners—one for each different surface in your office—you might find you only need one or two. This reduces your purchases and the amount of plastic packaging that ends up in landfills.

Reusing

To me, reusing feels like the middle sibling that is always forgotten. Often assumed to be the same as recycling, reusing is a completely different beast. Recycling is a manufacturing process while reusing extends the life of a product. For example, thrift stores are reusing rather than recycling. The benefits of reusing are enormous. It eliminates the need for other products. Carbon dioxide, methane, and toxins leaching into groundwater during decomposition are all things that happen in landfills and can be reduced via reusing.

Recycling

Recycling has a focus on raw materials rather than focusing on what the product can do. The most significant benefit of this process is that it reduces the need to extract more raw materials. Look at aluminum. Recycling aluminum uses only 9% of the energy needed to extract it from the ground. On a smaller scale, frequently referred to as down-cycling, products can change their function. An old shirt with holes that's turned into rags is a great example of this and has the benefit of reusing, reducing the need for paper towels.

There are two forms of recycling: internal and external recycling. Internal recycling is where the manufacturer takes what could be waste and finds a use for it to offset other costs. External recycling transfers the material to another organization to be reprocessed.

External recycling can be seen in companies like Terracycle. Terracycle, and similar companies, have waste that would usually be destined for the landfill shipped to their headquarters and their factory processes it, digging through the waste for content that can be recycled into new products and material. Coffee pods are cleaned of grounds, which are turned into fertilizer. The plastic pods themselves, as well as chip packets from school lunches and other plastics, become park benches.

One aspect of recycling to keep in mind is that it masks a deeper issue. Just because a company is diverting waste from the landfill doesn't mean that waste practices are up to par. A recycling rate of 75% is fantastic but because recycling is not the answer to the global environmental crisis, you must also consider how to reduce waste completely.

PRO TIP: Reduce waste bins and increase recycling bins. This will discourage people from putting everything into one bin, divide waste appropriately, and reduce the amount of landfill waste that they bring into the building.

SECTION III

SUSTAINABILITY DRIVING FINANCIAL CHANGE

If you and your company want more of a sustainability challenge, the following chapters explore how to do that.

These are all generally projects that have long-term impacts, though how long they take will depend on you, as there will be an element of overcoming fear of the unknown, especially in the fields of technology and finance. In my experience, no one wants to deal with finances until it's absolutely necessary, but you will have to in order to make these big changes. Our world is dictated by finance and the economy. To date, that has been to the detriment of our planet, but by tackling these issues head on, you contribute to expanding ripple effects of sustainability.

While Section II focused on projects and implementing sustainability goals that directly affect your business, this section is more about how you can effect change in degrees of separation away from you and your business. This is about taking control of your power to increase your scope of influence.

Eleven

Carbon Footprints and Environmental Audits

Y ou've heard the term carbon footprint, but do you know what it means? Do you know why it's profitable to reduce it? Does your company measure its carbon footprint and have targets set to reduce its impact? If not, get ready to formulate your carbon footprint reduction plan. In this chapter, we are going to break down some types of sustainable audits that can save the planet and keep your bank account healthy, too.

Carbon Footprint: What Is It?

Calculating your carbon footprint is a great tool to figure out where to target your business's first environmental efforts. A business's carbon footprint is the greenhouse gases (often measured in carbon dioxide) that are emitted during the course of its operations. It's basically the impact a business has on climate change. A common misconception is that carbon dioxide is the only greenhouse gas we should be worried about, but in fact, there are six greenhouse gases identified as responsible for climate change. These are:

1. Carbon dioxide (CO_2)
2. Methane (CH_4)
3. Nitrous oxide (N_2O)
4. Hydrofluorocarbons (HFCs)
5. Perfluorocarbons (PFCs)
6. Sulphur hexafluoride (SF_6)

The above greenhouse gases are identified by the Greenhouse Gas Protocol (ghgprotocol.org). Note that businesses need to make efforts to reduce all of these greenhouse gases, especially **methane** and **nitrous oxide,** as these are respectively 34 times and 298 times more destructive to the environment than carbon dioxide. Reducing methane can be as simple as composting, as this diverts between 5% and 15% of methane emissions because it allows organic waste to decompose properly and return to the earth to rejuvenate the soil.

Nitrous oxide, commonly known as laughing gas, is mainly used in the medical and dentistry industries. It is also a by-product of the automotive industry, is used as packaging filler for food, and can be found in aerosol cans. It is critical that we eliminate further nitrous oxide emissions as they contribute to the ozone layer thinning. If your business is in any of the above industries, it is a high priority to find solutions to eliminate these emissions immediately.

Hydrofluorocarbons contain fluorine and hydrogen and are frequently used in refrigerators and air conditioners. According to Project Drawdown, they are the world's greatest source of greenhouse gas emissions, due to the lack of regulation and recycling in their disposal process and their increased use due to rising global temperatures. Hydrofluorocarbons are also thousands of times worse than carbon dioxide with regard to global warming impact.

Perfluorocarbons or perfluoroalkanes are used in refrigerants, anesthetics, and aluminum smelting, which is the major contributor to this potent greenhouse gas. They have low-boiling points and a long atmospheric lifespan, so are hard to remove once they are in the atmosphere.

Sulfur hexafluoride, an extremely potent greenhouse gas, is an excellent electrical insulator, so it is mostly used in the electrical and medical industries. According to the Intergovernmental Panel on Climate Change (IPCC), these greenhouse gases have 23,900 times more warming potential than carbon dioxide and have the potential to stay in the atmosphere for up to 3,200 years.

Some of these greenhouse gases may not be relevant to your business unless you are in specific industries, but most businesses these days have some kind of refrigerator and/or air conditioning unit. When reviewing your carbon footprint, make sure to consider all the potential greenhouse gases in your business, as some of the lesser known will have a far more potent effect than carbon dioxide itself.

Calculate Your Carbon Footprint

For the most part, calculating your carbon footprint can be done through online carbon calculators, especially if you've never done one before. Carbonfund.org has a great tool for businesses to calculate carbon emissions, considering the needs of small to large offices. Using North American averages, Carbonfund.org calculates your greenhouse gas emissions and the cost to offset them. You can include these amounts in your finances and reporting, which will help prioritize areas emitting the most greenhouse gases. Evaluating your impact on the environment allows you to identify areas to improve. To reduce your impact, there are a few key environmental performance indicators:

- Energy consumption
- Water consumption
- Fuel use for business travel
- Paper purchased
- Total garbage, recyclables, and composted waste
- % of ENERGY STAR-rated electronics and appliances
- % of green-certified office products

Calculating your carbon footprint is, in part, the measuring of greenhouse gas emissions resulting from your office's operations. This includes carbon dioxide, methane, and nitrogen oxides. Activities are not just those done in your office building, but those of your suppliers and distributors. For example, paper doesn't just appear out of thin air. Even recycled paper needs to go through a processing plant that consumes an extraordinary amount of energy and water. A portion of that can be attributed to a ream of paper. Or look at transportation. The plant that manufactured your car did the same thing. You get the idea.

The additional information you need to calculate your carbon footprint:
1. Invoices
2. Usage amounts for energy, gas, fuel, water, electricity
3. Time dedicated to inputting values into a carbon calculator

Once you have your carbon footprint, analyze your findings and discuss them with others in your company. These findings may need to be translated into meaningful language or comparisons like, "This is the same amount of carbon that 100 cars use per year/month/day." You may even consider publishing it on the Environmental Protection Agency's Climate Leaders or the Carbon Disclosure Project.

However, the most important thing to do with your carbon footprint information is to identify areas for improvement. Which areas in your business have the largest climate impact? Why? Once you know those areas, your business can turn to maximizing efficiency. Being as efficient and minimal-waste as possible is the best way to reduce your carbon footprint and environmental impact. If your facilities are energy efficient and minimize material wastes, then replacing current fossil fuel energy with renewable energy will be more financially sensible for the long-term health of your business.

Breaking Down Greenhouse Gases

Greenhouse gas emissions are measured based on four emission types called scopes. These are:

SCOPE ONE: DIRECT EMISSIONS

These are greenhouse gases that directly correlate to the burning of fossil fuels or powering vehicles or other equipment. This includes emissions from chemical reactions or the decomposition of organic materials in composting, or fugitive emissions (leaks).

SCOPE TWO: INDIRECT EMISSIONS

These emissions are from electricity use. Almost every single person and business uses electricity through powering equipment, heating, and lighting. If this electricity comes from a mainline, as in not produced on-site, then the carbon dioxide and other greenhouse gases emitted in the power plant stations must be factored into the footprint.

SCOPE THREE: THIRD-PARTY INDIRECT EMISSIONS

All businesses work with vendors or suppliers that have their own carbon footprint comprised of direct and indirect emissions from electricity and additional indirect emissions. The emissions of vendors and suppliers need to be calculated into your carbon footprint. This includes not just the electricity used to generate or create the product or service they sold to you, but also the emissions used to deliver it to you if it's a physical product.

This brings us back to the importance of suppliers because they are impacting your business, and your world, in an unexpected way.

You would also include your employees' emissions here, such as their commute to your office and any emissions they would use in their home office if you support telecommuting in your company. Home office emissions would include energy, water, waste, and heating bills, as well as ventilation and indoor air quality, if you're really ambitious.

SCOPE FOUR: DOWNSTREAM INDIRECT EMISSIONS

These emissions tend to be two or three degrees of separation away from your direct actions. They are generated from the use of products and/or services you provide. These would be the emissions generated by your customers in the use of your product or service and in the disposal of your product. For example, if you sell a food product, that would include the emission used in refrigeration or cooking it, and the potential methane if it is thrown into a landfill. Or if you sell electronics or paper products, you would calculate the emissions used to power the electronics and the methane created by the paper product in the landfill.

Scope four is not always included when calculating a business's carbon footprint due to its complexity and the need to rely on assumptions, but I encourage you to do so (maybe once your company has a handle on scopes one to three). Puma included scope four in their environmental profit and loss, which was where most of their emissions came from and is the approach *Cradle to Cradle* authors William McDonough and Michael Braungart advocate—that a business is responsible for its product through its entire lifecycle from conception to production to disposal. The absolute minimum required to measure an accurate business carbon footprint is to measure scopes one, two, and three. This will capture the environmental impact of your entire organization, providing you with a true picture of your environmental impact.

Limiting Scope

Where you stop is an issue raised in measuring the scope of a business's indirect emission. Measuring a product's entire lifecycle, via the cradle-to-cradle approach, can be overwhelming. But there are shortcuts. The following are from Gareth Kane's *The Three Secrets of Green Business*:

- **80/20 thinking:** If your company consumes a large amount of energy-intensive material (e.g., aluminum) and a tiny amount of low energy services (e.g., contractors who carry out an annual site audit), then it is reasonable to include the production of aluminum and exclude the contractors.
- **Use of published data:** If your suppliers already publish their carbon footprint, then it is reasonable to use a pro rata amount of this. If you can find data from a study on a similar organization, you can use that as long as you document the source and the justification for using it.

The next step is plugging your data into a spreadsheet and creating a central place for all your information and assumptions to be made available. Your spreadsheet can have separate tabs for research, your internal office data, financials, carbon footprint, etc. You will also need a list of your suppliers and their addresses, which is hopefully easy to find. (If not, this could indicate an operational efficiency.)

Making Assumptions

As you can see, calculating your carbon footprint is complicated. Inevitably, assumptions will need to be made, as Gareth Kane explains in his book, *The Three Secrets of Green Business*. With any business metrics, especially KPIs, the important information is how you support the way you came to these conclusions. A few assumptions to measure your carbon footprint are the anticipated life of your product, how your consumers will use it, what portion of your suppliers' footprint is connected to your product, etc.

The challenge of life cycle assumptions is that you can't predict the future. It is hard to anticipate what product uses will be, especially with new products. Items can become economically obsolete, like the fax machine, before the product begins to physically malfunction. And then there are others that are indestructible.

Another tool to use for calculating your carbon footprint is nationally-accepted data. For example, the UK uses 0.43kg CO_2 per unit for electricity. Again, these numbers could change as more information regarding impact comes to light. The general rule is to be conservative and assume numbers that make your footprint larger, rather than smaller. And one more element: Be transparent. How you calculate your numbers shouldn't be hidden. Transparency allows others in your industry to learn and your company can receive feedback on ways to improve.

Assumptions can be tested using sensitivity analysis. The data arising from the assumption is changed by a small amount and its influence on the results measured. Assumptions that may cause wide swings in results can be analyzed further to ensure accuracy and to make sure you are not over- or under-estimating your carbon footprint.

Once you've maximized the efficiency of your business's operations and converted to renewable energy, offsetting carbon emissions or joining a carbon trading program is the next step.

How to Perform a Sustainability Audit

A sustainability audit is similar to a financial or tax audit, except that it focuses on ways your business impacts the environment. You may find the information below to be generic, but that is intentional, as the point of a sustainability audit is to critically examine your business and see if there are improvements to be made, small or large. Compared to a financial audit, which is very quantitative and contained, sustainability focuses much more on qualitative data and behavioural impact, which varies significantly from company to company. A sustainability audit usually includes actionable outcomes to reduce your carbon footprint as an end-product. You break your business into sections, such as:

- Purchasing
- Operating
- Waste removal
- Hazardous waste removal
- Energy use
- Water use
- Land use

This is a non-exhaustive list, and you can also include subsections for calculating your scope one to three emissions in each of these sections. The important thing to focus on first is the areas or processes that will have the most impact. Your employees will usually be able to contribute to a sustainability audit to ensure you are focusing on the most effective processes of your business. There may be some overlap between these sections in your business. For example, your daily operations usually involve using energy to keep the lights on. If you deliver products to your customers though, that will be included in the operating section but not the energy section.

Once you have the sections laid out, you answer questions like:
- Do we have any environmental or social policies in place regarding this area of our business?
- Are we being as efficient as possible? Are there behavioral practices that are contributing to wasted energy, productivity, water, etc.?

- What makes up the money spent in this sector? Are these expenditures necessary?
- What greenhouse gases are produced by this process?
- Does our business have a positive or negative effect on these gases and resources?

You would look through each sector, diving into its finances and processes to see whether your business is being as efficient as possible. You would ask for feedback from the various stakeholders in your business, particularly external ones like suppliers or consumers, as they will bring their external knowledge, which could spark innovation.

Hazardous waste is an important section to remember, as this includes things like paint and batteries, which might not be central to your business, but it is incredibly important to dispose of them responsibly. Generally, batteries are not recyclable and toxic if thrown into the garbage, so it is important to seek out the correct way to dispose of these items and make sure everyone in your office knows the procedure.

Implementing this would be the process part of the audit. Researching possible hazardous wastes and finding what might be applicable to your business. Asking questions about how these hazardous waste products are disposed of, researching how it is possible in your area, and then informing and educating your staff to ensure this process is followed in the future.

Depending on your business and what makes sense for your situation, there are a variety of different potential outcomes. Your business can implement a waste program that will ensure these products are recycled safely. Or you may decide to buy reusable batteries. Or you might partner with the supplier of paint to return unused portions that they can then use for samples or sell at a discount. There are endless possibilities, and the solutions will present themselves when you ask your stakeholders. Don't be afraid to turn to the internet for inspiration either, as this can also provide you with location- or industry-specific solutions. You can also use the B Corporation assessment tool for inspiration and guidance.

Green Audit Changes

After your green audit, it will be clear where gains can be made. Next is to look at the changes to be made. Here are changes, both easy and hard, to implement. You can also refer to books like *Greening Your Office* or *The Green Business Guide* that can provide more examples and ideas for your specific business situation. Below are some low hanging fruit changes that can yield savings quickly.

BUILDING AND OPERATIONS

- At night, turn off all lights, except for emergency lights
- Set computers and monitors to sleep when not in use
- Install motion sensors in low traffic areas such as washrooms, hallways, storage spaces, or promote staff habits of turning off lights with signage
- Set thermostats to lower temperatures for unoccupied spaces
- Replace conventional hand dryers and paper towels with hand towels or energy efficient hand dryers
- Upgrade kitchen appliances and office equipment to ones that are EN-ERGY STAR certified
- Replace lightbulbs with LED or fluorescent tube lighting
- Purchase laptops, monitors, and computers that are TCO certified computers and ENERGY STAR certified
- Insulate hot water tanks and piping
- Replace windows with ones that are double-paned or draft-proofed. Install a draft seal on all outdoor entrances and exits
- Purchase renewable energy credits from Bullfrog (or a similar company) for 100% of energy use to be carbon neutral

TRANSPORTATION

- Provide bicycle parking for staff and clients to encourage green transportation
- Encourage staff via incentives to commute by bike, transit, carpooling, or walking

- Use video or voice conferencing technology to minimize travel to and from meetings
- Contract local couriers and delivery services that use low or zero emission transport such as bikes, EV hybrids, electric cars, etc.
- Ensure company-owned vehicles are low- or zero-emission models

WATER

- Use tap water instead of bottled. Ban bottled water from office parties and events, opting to use pitchers instead
- Ensure all faucets use less than or equal to six litres per minute aerators
- Ensure all toilets use less than or equal to six litres per flush and urinals equal to or less than 1.9 litres per use

PURCHASING AND PRODUCTS

- Discontinue purchasing single-use kitchen products such as coffee cartridges, sugar packages, stir sticks, etc. Replace single-use products like paper cups, plates, cutlery, etc. with sustainable options.
- Purchase cleaning products that are eco-friendly
- Select caterers who are actively committed to sustainability
- Purchase office stationery supplies that contain at least 30% post-consumer recycled content
- Purchase used office equipment, such as printers and copiers, instead of new
- Use TerraCycle programs for hard to recycle material

WASTE

- Set all printers to print double-sided and use both sides of the page before recycling
- Create paperless systems, such as digitally storing invoices, newsletters, memos, and receipts
- Recycle all paper, cardboard, glass, tin, as well as soft and rigid plastic
- Establish infrastructure for organic waste

CLIMATE ACTION

- Carbon emissions are measured and reduction plan targets established and communicated to staff and public
- Offset emissions with certified carbon credits

Waste Minimization and Recycling

Whenever you read about reducing waste or your carbon footprint in your business, the first piece of advice is often to conduct energy, water, and waste audits, but what does that mean?

For a waste audit, it basically means getting into the nitty-gritty, going through your garbage to see what's in there and how it got there. If you were to look into the garbage right now, what would you see? Are there excessive tea or cookie wrappers that have come from individually wrapped snacks? Are there plastics and papers that could be recycled? Does organic waste go in the garbage or get separated out? Keep in mind that there are likely companies or community groups in your area that would love your compostable waste. Creating a separate bin for things that are compostable is easy and can make a huge reduction in your carbon footprint.

Ask your local municipality if they have compost available privately, if not publicly. Twenty-three percent of total waste is compostable, contributing significantly to methane gas output. Composting can be a huge decrease in your waste and footprint, but many complain that fruit flies and odour deter them from this activity. If you're emptying the bin every one to three days, you'll avoid the smell. Keep compost bin seals airtight when the lid is closed to keep flies away. Store fruit in containers or fridge instead of on counters to decrease the flies' food sources. You can do the same with your compost, creating a fridge or freezer system that slows down decomposition. If fruit flies are still an issue, set a wine bottle on the counter and fill it one-quarter full with red wine vinegar—all the flies will fly in and die.

Make sure to put compostable bags in your bin. They should be more than just biodegradable, as those are still made from plastic. Look for bags made from cornstarch or other plant-based material.

Here is one way to record your waste audit:

MY COMPANY'S WASTE AUDIT

Location: Print Room	Location
Bin size: 10 gallons	Bin size (L/Gal/m3)
Fill frequency: Weekly	Fill frequency
Nonrecyclable content • Misc. food wrappers Approx. %: 10%	Nonrecyclable content
Recyclable content: • Paper • Plastic Approx. %: 80%	Recyclable content
Organic content • Food: fruit peels Approx. %: 10%	Organic content Approx. %

Source: David Suzuki's *Green Guide*

Table 8 Example of Waste Audit

The best way to minimize waste is to stop it from coming through your door. It's easier to avoid products than deal with the waste once it is in your supply chain. Waste usually comes into the business from what is bought. Packaging is part of all purchases, so be mindful of what you're buying. Choose items that have less packaging and buy in bulk when appropriate. Buy office snacks that are not individually wrapped, and stationery that is FSC or otherwise responsibly and sustainably sourced.

If you are a solopreneur or small business with under five employees, consider doing a zero waste challenge. This is a great way to become aware of what you're paying for that ends up in the garbage without having to go through your garbage en masse, which you may prefer if the idea of going through garbage grosses you out. The idea of a zero waste challenge is to become aware of what everyday items you throw out and find ways to avoid doing so, either by reusing or refusing. This can be done by changing how something is purchased, not buying it in the first place, or creating a packaging return agreement, which is fairly common in manufacturing with pallets or containers.

You can sign up for zero waste challenges online. There are a few blogs that have also written about experiences of going through a zero waste challenge. Find one that is coming up or that is located near your part of the world as they will be able to give you insights into your situation. For example, if your municipality does not have recycling and compost collection, your business may have to get creative with how it manages incoming and outgoing waste.

I completed a zero waste challenge last year, and though I didn't do as well as the organizer, I was happy with how well I did in that month. Since the challenge, I've noticed an increased awareness of what I put in my garbage can and what isn't recyclable. Now, I try to reuse containers if I know they're immediately going into the garbage. But the biggest takeaway has been to eat fewer unhealthy snack foods because they come with so much packaging! Also, I switched to loose leaf teas because I drink a lot of tea and throwing away a wrapper adds up by the time I've gone through an entire box. Loose leaf teas can be entirely composted, and their original containers can be recycled. Zero waste, here I come!

Energy Audit

We've talked a lot about energy, becoming efficient in it, and how it will save your business money. Now it's time to create a plan to make your own business more efficient. Once you know the changes you want to implement, put together a plan for change. As an entrepreneur, you are an excellent planner, but here are some things to consider.

An energy audit would take place over an extended period of time, several weeks ideally, so that you get a good sampling of everyday behaviour. You may need to conduct audits in winter and summer, if practices and costs of day-to-day operations change widely between these two seasons. Similar to waste and water audits, it is important to notice how energy is being used in your office and, more importantly, wasted. It could be as simple as having a sheet of paper filled with questions and space for checkmarks or to fill in answers. Recording these things are important because you might not realize how often they happen or how much it costs you without documenting it.

The first phase of the energy audit is to collect your data. This data will come from your energy bills. Some energy providers will allow you to access this data online and to compare your use year over year. You will need the cost and energy used by month, as the baseline.

The next stage is to break down your energy usage by item, department or location, whichever makes the most sense for your company. In most small businesses, you will need to know how much electricity is used by machines versus computers versus appliances, so you would break down the usage by item.

If your energy provider breaks down your usage into type, it will make this next stage easier. If not, you will need to do some math. You would plug your usage numbers into a spreadsheet (example below) to see where your energy goes. In the example below, appliances generate almost 50% of the energy used. This is important to know as it could indicate a number of things, like it is not sealing properly, it is not a good quality appliance, or there is a problem with it and it needs to be fixed or replaced.

Once you've investigated the biggest use of your energy, you move onto the next. In the above example, it is running machines, and if you are in an office, it would be concerning if your machines are using more energy than your computers. You would want to find out why. Perhaps it's because they're always left on. Perhaps your machinery needs to be serviced, as it is not running optimally.

The next step in your audit would be to investigate your heating and air conditioning usage. First, you would determine if the energy used is comparable to other buildings. You should also check to see if the energy used is similar to the averages for the model of air conditioner or heater you have. If it is not, your unit may need to be serviced or the filters changed.

My Company Energy Audit				
Operating expense savings	Energy Usage (kWh)	% Total	Energy Cost ($0.18/kWh)	Carbon Emissions (CO_2 kg)
Total Energy Usage 2019	5,000.00	100%	$900.00	155.00
Machines (running as printers, projectors, telephones, would count as machines in an office)	1,650.00	33%	$297.00	51.15
Appliances (Fridge, Microwave, Boiler, Oven, etc.)	2,350.00	47%	$423.00	72.85
Computers and Electronics	900.00	18%	$162.00	27.90
Heating/Cooling	100.00	2%	$18.00	3.10
Notes				
Keep notes regarding the energy audit here or in comments, particularly around any assumptions used or sources for the data used. E.g. Carbon emissions calculated from Bullfrog averages. Cost of Energy 2019 Toronto Hydro average of Mid-Peak and Peak rates (20.8+14.4)/2. Carbon Emissions calculated using Ontario Annual Average Emissions Factor 31g/kWh				

Figure 4 Table Example of an Energy Audit

What you might find is that the units are left on overnight, heating or cooling a building with no one in it. This is a huge waste of energy, as evenings and weekends should be when you see a minimal amount of energy usage from these air conditioners or heaters. If you find this to be the case, it is likely worth investing in a programmable thermostat. Installing one of these will give you peace of mind that you are never wasting money on heating an empty building, as you can program it to automatically turn off on the weekends and in the evening. The beauty with these programmable thermostats is that they can be overridden or changed if you need to work in the office late or your office hours change for any reason.

The last step from the above example would be to look into electronics, as they account for the least amount of your energy use. According to Resource Nation, the majority of energy use by computers happens when people are not sitting in front of them, either because they are in meetings or carrying out their daily duties. You can easily implement an office policy and make sure to remind your employees to change their computer settings so that the screen turns off after fifteen minutes of inactivity and goes to sleep after thirty. Encourage folks to set computers to shut down overnight.

You do not have to follow this order if you have preliminary information or if it is easier to investigate specific areas of your business. Starting with what you know is an important first step forward. Perhaps you already know that electronics are left on all the time and want to calculate whether the savings from buying and installing a TrickleStar power bar are worthwhile.

Once you have identified potential problems, you would then compare the energy use after implementing changes to see how much energy was saved. You can plan to use these saved funds to invest into bigger projects next year that might reduce waste. Or you could use the saved funds to replace old machines or equipment, recycling the old ones where possible, of course.

Implementing Changes

Change is inevitable, and entrepreneurs need to be able to change as business changes. Once you've done some of the audits outlined above, you may find a need to change multiple processes or things in your business, or need to retrain staff to do things more efficiently. Implementing these changes won't always be easy, but nothing ever is. Here are some tips to help ease the transition.

- **Create a timeline:** Change needs to occur at a continual yet comfortable pace. Overnight changes are hard to sustain, so prioritizing and putting changes in place via stages will increase the likelihood of success.
- **Celebrate the wins:** With fast-paced work environments, we forget to give credit for our successes. Celebrate your progress each year and instill a sense of pride for environmental changes. Reflect on your baseline assessment and see how far you've come. Reward the team's efforts!
- **Communicate progress:** Those involved should be informed of new changes, actions, or challenges along the way. Depending on your needs, monthly or quarterly reports would communicate the journey. Choosing a few Key Performance Indicators (KPIs) to measure success will allow clear reports on progress. How much waste has been diverted? How much energy has been saved? Using real numbers will provide quantitative measurements about which your employees can feel good. Set targets and monitor how well you're doing.
- **Create incentives:** Reward the office when you reach your targets. Gift certificates to local, sustainable businesses or B Corps or staff field trips are some suggestions, but you know your employees best. Ask them what they want and give it to them. You can also reward staff for commuting via public transport or carpooling by reimbursing their expenses.

What's Next?

Several countries have introduced a carbon tax or a carbon trading program. This is a tax on the amount of carbon dioxide, or equivalents of methane and other greenhouse gases, used in your business. In other words, this is a tax on the environmental impact of your business. Many companies are choosing to voluntarily track their carbon footprint, as they know regulation will require it sooner than later. This alone will reduce future compliance costs, as they will not need to hire experts or train staff to understand carbon footprint accounting within a set timeline. The best part about calculating your carbon footprint is that it decreases direct costs moving forward. It identifies areas where you can do better and improves your bottom line.

Carbon offsetting is popular with environmentally-friendly companies. There are many companies, like Bullfrog Power, that sell carbon credits to offset the carbon generated from a flight or that was used in generating electricity for your business. Bullfrog Power then invests this money in renewable energy projects, building solar and wind farms across the country to accelerate the adoption of renewable energy in Canada. This is not a unique business model and is done in other countries such as in the UK, the U.S., Australia, China, and India.

Going one step further on this environmental journey is carbon insetting. Essentially, it's the process of planting trees in agroforestry systems, which use crop farmland to plant trees and shrubs between rows, allowing for biodiversity and to offset erosion. This activity is gaining popularity, particularly among European brands such as Chanel, Nespresso, and L'Oréal, because it allows companies to build resiliency in their supply chains and restore ecosystems on which their growers depend. Insetting takes a holistic approach, tackling both environmental and social challenges, which is largely poverty among smallholder farmers. The article "L'Oreal, Chanel and Nespresso Pioneer 'Carbon Insetting'" outlines that:

> *Nespresso has embarked on a massive initiative with a principal architect of insetting, PUR Project, planting 10 million trees in Colombia, Guatemala, Ethiopia, Mexico and Nicaragua to reach carbon neutrality by 2020. Nespresso is investing $600 million over five years in the initiative because it sees insetting as a "virtuous cycle," said its French division president, Arnaud Deschamps. "You plant trees to offset your emissions. You help your farmers with better land, better ecosystems and better revenues, so their children want to be farmers too. And we upgrade the coffee quality for our consumers." (Wilcox, 2017)*

Your business can commit to this in several ways, depending on your situation. One is to donate a percentage of revenue or profits to an organization already planting trees in your area. By partnering with them, they are able to access more funding, which is needed to plant more trees, and your company is committing to reducing its carbon footprint.

Your business could also set up a volunteer day, where you can partner with a local tree planting organization. I would personally advise partnering with an organization already doing tree planting if they exist in your area, as they will know best about what is needed for the local ecosystem. But if such an organization doesn't exist where you are, you can create a workday in the spring or summer to go out and plant trees. Your company would pay for local trees, and your employees would plant them for interested homeowners or in public parks, if your local government permits it.

Depending on whether you own your building site, you could commit to planting native trees and plants on your property. This is especially important in areas that are highly industrial, where there is little else to offset rainwater runoff or the heat island effect. If your business is buying or building a building, you could commit to working with an architect who can help with installing a green roof or designing the building in such a way that allows for vines or moss to cover it.

Carbon insetting leads to another term, ecological footprinting, which expresses environmental impact based on the area required by your operations. Gareth Kane goes into further detail in his book, *The Three Secrets of Green Business*, but usually ecological footprinting is calculated with the following:

- The land taken up by buildings and physical infrastructure, such as roads, to support the creation and supply of your service or product
- The land required to produce food, fibre, and forestry products
- The theoretical amount of forested land required to recycle all our carbon dioxide emissions back into oxygen

For many businesses, land use is not a major environmental issue compared to their other impacts. If your business has a focus on food, forest, fibre, and other such products, then your ecological footprint may be a more thorough indicator than carbon footprint. This is because it measures the use of biologically productive land and water, all of which are finite resources.

Measuring the environmental impacts of your business through products and services is essential to managing your impact and communicating it to your stakeholders. If you are in the food, fibre, or forestry industry, start with an ecological footprint measurement, and all other industries can begin to measure their carbon footprint. Enhance your carbon footprint calculation with direct measurements such as waste sent to landfill and water consumption, to focus on actionable steps.

Also, remember that measuring your impact is not the same as being eco-friendly. Once you have measured your business impacts, it's time to put a plan into action to begin reducing them.

Twelve

Where Do You Invest Your Money?

Ethical Investments

Investing your retirement money and savings into ethical investments is about using your money to ignite change. Your company has a mission to be a force of good, and this should be reflected in how you spend and invest your money. Ethical and impact investments are a perfect vehicle to start change. As an investor, you have the ability to impact stock prices, which managers of big companies care about deeply. Because how and what you purchase is a form of voting, savvy investing in ways that accelerate renewable energy, environmental technologies, and promote responsible business practices is a powerful way to increase your company's impact. Not to mention, the global Green Economy has now surpassed $8.1 trillion and is a rapidly growing sector of investment.

To start the change, write a quick email to your financial advisor, your bank or 401K Fund record keeper, or your retirement fund manager, saying:

> *"I want to speak with you about the types of companies I'm investing in. I am concerned about the social and environmental impact of many large companies, and I want to make sure my money is not funding business practices I disagree with, such as toxic chemicals, arms, oil and petroleum, pornography, violent entertainment, heavy metals, GMO and non-organic food, and animal testing.*
>
> *If I have investments in these types of companies, I wish to discuss options to sell those and reinvest in renewable energy or other impact investment options."*

It may not be as easy as switching out of these funds to another if you are located in the U.S., as your employer and record keeper would need to work together to offer you funds that have gone through an environmental, social, and governance screen. This is still extremely rare in the U.S., but if you and your colleagues demand to be provided with an ethical 401K investment option, it will start the ball rolling. If you're an employer who provides a 401K and measures their scope one to four emissions, don't forget to include the emissions from your 401K. If your funds include fossil fuels, that may provide some motivation to remove yourself from those investments as they balloon your scope four emissions.

If you work directly with a financial advisor or fund manager, below are questions you can ask to find out more about what you are really investing in. This will start a dialogue with your financial advisor, who may not be aware of any of this information, but in the process of asking, you and your advisor may be shocked to learn what your retirement funds and savings are invested in.

Questions for your financial advisor to consider:

- Are these companies committed to reducing their environmental footprint?
- Have these companies met previous targets to reduce waste, water, or energy consumption?
- Are they audited regularly and make their financials available to the public?
- Do they have publicly available sustainability reports?
- Are they pursuing third party certifications to verify sustainability claims?
- Are the company's emissions and carbon footprint lower than others in its industry?
- Are employees paid a living wage, not just minimum wage, but more than enough to live in the city in which they are based?
- Do these companies prioritize their employees' well-being and work-life balance?
- What are they doing differently than others in their industry? How are they disrupting or innovating the market?

- If a company creates a product from raw materials (manufacturing, cosmetics, etc.), is there toxic waste, and how is it managed?
- How long do you intend to invest in these companies?

If you live in Canada, you can sell mutual funds or stocks that are invested inappropriately and instead invest in CoPower Green Bonds, which are funding solar installations and building retrofits to be more energy efficient.

Audrey Choi's TED Talk "How to Make a Profit While Making a Difference" has a lot to say regarding savings bonds and stock investments. Choi highlights an important point that of the $290 trillion in stocks and bonds, retirement funds and savings account for one third. The rest is controlled by institutions and corporations that are governed and answerable to us, the people, who can force them to make different financial choices at any time. If we choose to take on that power, we can make a difference.

You may already be choosing to take sustainable action with your everyday actions: buying organic and fair trade coffee, using reusable travel mugs that reduce landfill waste one disposable cup at a time, etc. As stated earlier in this book, our small collective actions contribute to a bigger picture. With ethical investments, we can have an even larger impact. Ethical investments are those stocks, mutual funds, and bonds that are common in traditional investing, with an added element of only investing in companies that are committed to environmental sustainability, social responsibility, and good governance. Many stock exchanges and government pension funds around the world require companies to issue statements on their social and environmental policies, such as in Norway and Australia.

There are also new and exciting ways for people to invest as the market continues to change. Community bonds are a growing investment sector, as are microloans. Community bonds are a shared investment where the opt-in amount is less than $1000, making the barrier to entry quite low. This is particularly attractive to young people or those who don't have a lot of extra cash to invest. These community bonds are then invested in community-based projects that will benefit an entire neighbourhood, like building a solar farm. They can also be used to build wind farms and micro-farms or fund small business growth.

The Centre for Social Innovation (CSI) used community bonds to great success in 2015 when they needed to raise capital to purchase their third property. Bonds were issued for members and the wider community to purchase with a three- or five-year maturity term. This allowed them to have more than a minimum down payment for the purchase of the building, lowering their overall mortgage and interest payments.

Microloans are a booming business in the developing world. There is a significant barrier for most people in the developing world to accessing cash. Microloans allow them to borrow, on average, $50. This doesn't sound like a lot, but it is enough to buy a goat or a beehive. This is the capital cost for someone to start their business selling milk or honey. This small loan gives individuals autonomy and bolsters the local economy. Individuals pay back the loan and then continue with their business. Kiva, a micro-financing company, has been doing this for ten years and has loaned over $937 million to people from Mexico, Brazil, Africa, and Asia. They've supported at least 3.2 million primarily female farmers grow their businesses. Microloans are critical support for women in developing countries, as Kiva lends 83% of its funds to women wanting to establish or grow their business in order to better support their family. This is better than a donation because it amplifies your contribution infinitely. These loans help people who would otherwise never have access to money because they cannot access fair and affordable sources of credit.

Water.org, based in Canada, is piloting similar projects around water sanitation with the same business model. Those who invest their extra money into the microloan program are able to reliably expect about a 3-4% return on investment. This is a higher return rate than at the bank and can be a safer investment than most stocks.

The Harvard Business School found investments in a portfolio of companies focused solely on profit generated half the returns of ethical companies. The ROI on those ethical investments doubled simply because they chose to protect the environment as well as make money. These companies engaged in initiatives outlined in previous chapters: monitoring energy and water usage to waste less and cut costs; taking a long-term approach to business growth; and building a work-life balance company culture that improved employee loyalty, retention, and productivity.

Let's break this down by looking at one such fund, the Parnassus Endeavor Institute Fund.

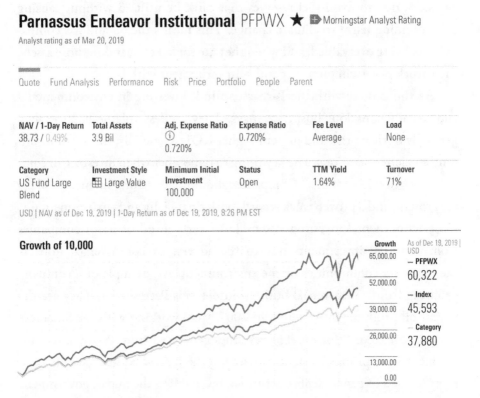

Parnassus Endeavor Institutional PFPWX ★ ➕Morningstar Analyst Rating

Analyst rating as of Mar 20, 2019

Quote Fund Analysis Performance Risk Price Portfolio People Parent

NAV / 1-Day Return	Total Assets	Adj. Expense Ratio	Expense Ratio	Fee Level	Load
38.73 / 0.49%	3.9 Bil	ⓘ 0.720%	0.720%	Average	None

Category	Investment Style	Minimum Initial Investment	Status	TTM Yield	Turnover
US Fund Large Blend	▦ Large Value	100,000	Open	1.64%	71%

USD | NAV as of Dec 19, 2019 | 1-Day Return as of Dec 19, 2019, 8:26 PM EST

Growth of 10,000

Growth	As of Dec 19, 2019 | USD
	— PFPWX
	60,322
	— Index
	45,593
	— Category
	37,880

65,000.00
52,000.00
39,000.00
26,000.00
13,000.00
0.00

Figure 5 ESG Fund growth compared to a conventional fund

This fund screens investments based on environmental, social, and governance (ESG) criteria similar to those mentioned in Choi's TED Talk and by the Harvard Business School. Below is a snapshot of their performance since 2009, and how $10,000 invested would have grown in the corresponding ten years.

If you had invested $10,000 in this fund back in 2009, that money would be worth $58,000 at the end of 2019. In contrast, investing that money in an ETF fund with low fees only nets you $44,450, and a conventional index fund yielded even less growth. In ten years, your retirement lost up to $21,000 because it was invested in fossil fuels or other companies that were not excluded for their environmental, social, and governance policies.

What conventional funds do not account for is the potential for stranded assets, due to fossil fuel reserves that can't be utilized without causing compounding harm to climate change. This means the oil and gas company's stocks are overvalued, and when they are forced to abandon those assets, their stock price will plummet and your retirement with it.

As you can see with the Parnassus fund, investing in environmentally and socially conscious businesses pays. They are less volatile because they generally mitigate risk and present higher ROIs. Generally, this is from running efficient operations. The key thing to remember when investing in companies is good governance. Companies should have strong financials, plans for growth, and a proven track record, both financially and environmentally.

Environmental investing also excludes certain industries or companies from potential investments due to the adverse or controversial impacts they have on communities or the environment. An example of a company profiting from controversial business interests is PetroChina. They are the largest oil producer in Asia and, in 2007, were working with the Sudanese government to drill for oil. The revenues generated from PetroChina's investment were primarily spent supporting the Janjaweed militia, who have been accused of genocide in Darfur. So, by enabling the Sudan government to finance its military oppression, PetroChina became directly financially responsible for contributing to the Darfur killings. How would you feel retiring on funds that were generated from genocide?

A general consensus is to avoid investing in companies that support, or are business partners or suppliers of companies involved in the following:

- Pornography
- Violent computer games or entertainment

- Arms and munitions, including guns and military arms
- Heavy metals, like mercury or lead
- Insecticides, pesticides, nanoparticles, and other toxins
- GMO and non-organic foods
- Oil and petroleum
- Animal testing

These are expanded below.

Pornography

Controversial to say the least, the restriction on investing in pornographic content is outside of porn being morally right or wrong.

If you are personally against pornography, then morally, you'll want to make sure you're not violating your principles through your investments. If you're not morally opposed to pornography, seek investments in companies that have shown strong leadership in caring for the health, safety, and education of their employees.

Violent Computer Games and Entertainment

While scaring yourself can be delightful, generally, violent video games are not good for overall public morale. This is not about whether violent video games contribute to gun violence or gender-based violence; it is about whether the final product helps consumers or not. Violent games and entertainment often desensitize individuals from suffering, due to overexposure. This is detrimental when we are currently in a time when public emotional investment is greatly needed. When the public feels disempowered and unable to do anything, they are far less likely to fix the current state of affairs.

Many games are also infamous for the toxicity of their online communities that normalize spewing hate, especially among young people. Some major game studios have taken steps to address these issues, to varying degrees of success, but they all continue to profit from these communities.

Investing in this sector may or may not personally or morally affect you, but, like making investments in pornography, you should be conscious about what the company is supporting. If video games are of specific interest to you, consider companies that make games you like or are intended to be light and engaging like Nintendo (who make Wii Fit) or The Pokemon Company. These are fun games that are profitable and aimed at children so have educational content threaded throughout.

Arms and Munitions

This goes without saying. If the market stops investing in weapons, there will be less capital to create products and less incentive for war.

Heavy Metals

Heavy metals such as lead, mercury, and cadmium are toxic and are considered poisons. They impact the health of millions globally, and those who engage in the manufacture and distribution of heavy metals are profiting today from tomorrow's medical bills.

Insecticides, Pesticides, Nanoparticles, and Other Toxins

In *Silent Spring*, Rachel Carlson described the damaging effects insecticides, pesticides, and other toxins have on not just the animal ecosystem but also on humans. She describes cases of people poisoning themselves, their children, and their pets due to the extensive use of insecticides and pesticides. These toxins are a huge drain on public finances and lead to long-term medical costs.

Unfortunately, since 1969, when her book was published, little has changed in the agriculture and gardening industries. Still, toxins are used, and although some are less harmful than those banned by the EPA due to *Silent Spring*, these products continue to adversely impact the environment, ecology, and biodiversity of the earth. Continual investment in these companies increases challenges for the growth of eco-friendly options in the market. Also, investment in companies that manufacture toxins increases overall medical costs. These companies have a limited future and will be pushed out of the marketplace as greater responsibility and accountability is required.

Pesticides are toxic to bees and lead to destroying the entire colony, even though crops depend on them for fertilization in order to bear fruit. For example, Chlorpyrifos is highly toxic to bees and is the most common pesticide used in the U.S. If you've purchased fresh food at the supermarket, it likely has traces of chlorpyrifos on it. While there is a lack of studies on its effects, it has been suggested that this pesticide negatively impacts the development of children's brains.

Most pesticides that are toxic to bees have not been banned, and you can probably buy them at your local department store. Every year folks buy pesticides to kill unwanted plants like dandelions or weeds, but these also kill bees and other animals integral to our environment.

GMO and Non-Organic Foods

GMO foods are banned in many countries around the world, notably in Europe. They are a hotly debated topic as the public has questioned their health benefits in developed countries. Generally, GMO crops tend not to be small farm friendly as the company producing the GMO seeds controls the patents for those seeds. Monsanto, purchased by Bayer in 2018, has been involved in multiple controversies and legal actions regarding this issue. GMO crops also tend not to be environmentally-friendly, as they are designed in North America to be pesticide-resistant so farmers can pump ever-increasing amounts of poison into the ground, air, and water. As *Silent Spring* speaks to at length, this is disastrous for the environment on many levels.

Organic farms are generally better for the surrounding environment. This is because the farmer is letting the plants and soil run the show, rather than dominate the landscape and force it to work with excessive spraying and fertilizing. Conventional farming practices are not environmentally efficient or friendly. Local forests are cut down to make way for mono-crops, decreasing local biodiversity and increasing the likelihood of pests and damage caused by storms. Over time, this also has negative impacts on the soil and surrounding wildlife.

Oil and Petroleum

Generally, mining is bad for the environment. Extracting raw material is extremely carbon intensive. However, some mining practices are worse than others. For example, the tar sands are a well-known example of a multi-faceted environmental disaster. Thousands of acres of forest have been destroyed, and refining the tar into usable petrol and shipping it increases fossil fuel usage. The fuel is then put into our cars, contributing to the climate crisis.

That alone is enough to show that the tar sands in Alberta are some of the worst oil mines in the world. Mining negatively contributes to climate change in a compounding way because:

- Extracting oil and petroleum damages the environment by cutting down a complex wild ecosystem, especially open pit mining, like the tar sands
- Fossil fuels, which are being extracted, are burned to obtain these new resources, creating a production catch-22
- Vast quantities of water and energy are used in the mining process
- To turn the tar sands into useable oil, an energy-intensive process is required, burning more fossil fuels
- It requires more fossil fuels to ship the refined oil to the market
- The oil is then used by consumers, adding to the carbon dioxide in the atmosphere

As you can see, mining new resources is far more environmentally damaging in the long term than recycling. Although you can't recycle fossil fuels, generally recycling reduces the use of fossil fuels by half.

Animal Testing

Animal testing has likely been around for as long as human society. There have been references to animal testing found in ancient Greece, and Aristotle himself performed experiments on animals. In more recent history, there as been a moral debate about the ethics of experimenting on animals, though this debate has been happening since the 1600s.

Cosmetic testing is particularly controversial and still legal in the United States. L'Oreal has been particularly vocal about its opposition to the animal testing ban in Europe, where its headquarters are located. This is because they consistently test their products on animals. Social attitudes generally lean towards protecting animals, and this is true for polls conducted showing that more than 50% of folks are morally opposed to animal testing. Yet, your retirement funds may be invested in a cosmetic or research company that tests on animals. L'Oreal is an obvious example as they are a well-known perpetrator of animal testing, but many other companies exist that are lesser known. Ask questions and do research about any companies in your portfolio to see if they test on animals, and you may find yourself needing to change your investments.

Ethical investments are not a new movement, but financial planners are still not savvy enough to identify good governance and sustainable efforts. So tell them about the kinds of companies you want to support and provide the above list as ones you don't want to invest in.

There are a variety of angles to consider when evaluating ethical investments. Some will be more important to you than others. Below is a comprehensive list of areas about which you can ask your advisor. For example, what does a potential investment opportunity do to alleviate poverty in developing nations? Other issues include:

- Respect for human rights
- Safe and healthy labour conditions
- Better health care benefits for workers
- Higher product safety standards
- Healthier food
- Low-impact farming
- Alleviating poverty in local communities or developing nations
- Animal rights
- Lower carbon and greenhouse gas emissions
- Preserving and advancing democracy

- Banning sales of weapons
- Avoiding sales of weapons to rogue/oppressive regimes
- Avoiding companies that profit from war (making army clothes, providing drone software)
- Not taking advantage of nicotine, alcohol, drugs, and gambling addictions
- Higher ethnic and gender diversity in corporate management
- Equal-opportunity employment
- Serving at-risk communities

Good governance is the practice of ensuring the company cares about more than profits. Safety and wellness practices for workers, environmental guidelines for manufacturing lines, and equal pay across the workforce create an environment for employees to thrive, while respecting the environment and providing benefits to shareholders. Many stock exchanges around the world now ask for public companies to include their governance practices or explain their lack of one, so investors are able to assess a company's long-term stability on more than just financial statements.

A company's governance standard also exposes risk. If, for example, the company is committed to the environment and has taken measures to reduce its carbon footprint, that company will likely be more profitable long-term and has a long-term vision to solving problems. For example, the Australian Securities and Investment Commission (ASIC), which regulates businesses in Australia, requires publicly-traded companies to disclose their environmental and social standards, in addition to meeting a standard of ethical guidelines. These include labour standards as well as environmental, social, or ethical considerations in selecting, retaining, and realizing an investment. This prevents greenwashing. Companies cannot just say they are committed to ensuring labour standards in their supply chain but must explain what standard they are using and why. This is important for companies that purchase goods from developing nations with less stringent labour laws such as India, China, Taiwan, and Cambodia. Developing nations have struggled with human rights in manufacturing, so the only way to ensure decent factory conditions is to hold the factory to western standards of health and safety.

There are other components to good governance, though they change based on industry and operations. Service-based companies, for instance, generally need less scrutiny regarding labour laws based on the education and location of their employees. But their transparency, environmental, and community commitments can be highly scrutinized. Some specific questions to ask your financial advisor around a company's good governance practices:

1. Is the company committed to reducing its environmental footprint?
2. Have they met previous targets to reduce waste and water/energy consumption?
3. Are they audited regularly and make their financials public?
4. Do they have publicly available sustainability reports?
5. Are they pursuing third party certifications to verify these sustainable claims? For example:
   i. B Corporation
   ii. LEED
   iii. Fair Trade
   iv. USDA Organic
6. Are the company's emissions and carbon footprint lower than others in its industry?
7. Are employees paid a living wage, one that is enough to live in the location where they are based?
8. Does the company prioritize its employee well-being and work-life balance?
   i. This can include initiatives like paid volunteer days; flextime; investing in green, eco-friendly workspaces; meditation or stress-busting workshops; paid education advancement; mentorships for women, etc.)
9. What are they doing differently than others in their industry? How are they disrupting or innovating the market?

i. This is especially important to consider in the health care industry, as pharmaceutical companies are generally not considered to be ethical investments due to lack of cooperation and poor work-life balance for employees. However, hospice care is usually an ethical investment.

10. If a company creates a product from raw materials (manufacturing, cosmetics, etc.), is there any toxic waste, and how is it managed?

    i. How are cosmetics or drugs tested?

    ii. Is there a waste reduction plan in place? Has the company hit previous targets?

11. How long do you intend to invest in these companies?

    i. This is particularly important because responsible investing is long-term investing. Wanting to invest in a company's growth helps prevent short-term missteps that often damage the environment, employees, and consumers.

This is a lot to take in, and many financial professionals will not have answers to the above questions. Unless your financial planner's specialty is ethical or sustainable investments, be wary of greenwashing. Having the above questions close at hand will allow you to see which companies present as green and which actually are. As you begin to ask these questions, it will increase the importance of these decisions.

These questions are designed to extract information about the larger ethical picture and provide you with appropriate information on if you should invest. External stakeholders are critically important to a company's survival, and if they are only thinking about themselves, it will become apparent.

Some questions are industry specific, so it can be difficult to know what to ask. Even those who work in manufacturing may operate differently than other manufacturing companies, depending on the product and location.

Generally, the thought process can be broken down into these steps:

• What is this company doing better and/or differently that benefits the environment?

- Overall, how does this industry impact the environment?
- How does this company treat employees? Is their well-being promoted within the company?
- Why is the company choosing to focus on specific initiatives? Is it the most effective and efficient investment?
- How does the company measure success regarding its environmental and social targets?

Remember that this will be a learning process. You may invest in a company that looks committed to ethical behaviour only to later discover that it isn't what it seemed. Investments can be moved, companies can change, and you can only do your best with the information provided.

Thirteen

How Technology Can Help Your Company Be More Green and Efficient

Technology is the steward of the future. Innovations in technology have allowed Western society to minimize carbon dioxide emissions and environmental impact. Unfortunately, there is resistance to adopting new technology and business processes. Canada and the U.S. use as many cheques as the developing world, whereas Europe and Australia have been pioneers in paperless systems and implementing new technology.

Reluctance to adopt tech-friendly processes is indicative of the "but we've always done it this way" attitude that is pervasive in North America. Small- and medium-sized businesses are known as nimble, adaptive enterprises in university circles, yet in my experience, small businesses have been reluctant to embrace technology.

This is in part because technology is changing so rapidly that it is nearly impossible to keep up with the latest and greatest developments. Installing software upgrades or buying a new computer can cause compatibility issues with your current system, which is frustrating and costly as a business owner. Another barrier is lack of knowledge or understanding—you may be comfortable with older technology because you understand it. This does not make it more secure and is likely a source of inefficiency in your business.

Creating a paperless office is more accessible than ever before, and yet most businesses haven't changed their processes to keep up with the advancements in technology. File storage solutions on a local network tend to require an IT professional for installation and maintenance, and is only successful if everyone in your organization uses it. There's no use in buying an online customer management system, for example, if some folks in your office are still working out of their address books.

There is an abundance of apps and online-storage solutions that can help with storing copies of your paperwork online, and companies like Amazon, Google, Dropbox, and Sync.com offer cheap solutions to store your information online securely. No longer do you need an all-in-one printer, scanner, fax machine. Your smartphone can be turned into a scanner, and if it can access documents online from anywhere at any time, there is no need for a printer.

To learn more about how technology could help small businesses, I spoke with Graham Binks, CEO of primeFusion Inc., about common challenges and solutions. Graham helps bring modern tech solutions to established small businesses and educates his clients about technology best practices. He shared with me some important factors to consider in your data storage as a small business.

Binks suggests a general rule: the eco-friendly IT solution for small- to medium-sized businesses is the cloud. By cloud, he means converting all processes and switching all data storage to an online-based company. These online companies have data centres (buildings filled with hard drives, essentially) where your information is stored and backed up on an ongoing basis.

The Importance of Data Security

Data security has very little to do with the equipment's physical location. What is much more important is the business's attitude towards the security of information. Ask yourself this question: What happens if this information gets out? If you store your business's finances, it is not ideal for that information to be stolen but, in the context of the bigger picture, that's not as important as securing customer credit card information. High risk situation: If you have a large enough volume of sensitive data transactions, like thousands or hundreds of thousands of consumers, then you could become a target for a hacker. They could breach your security, steal that information, and, if it's a large amount, put it on the black market, which could significantly harm your business. The important piece of this is that you can be sued if private information is stolen. That potential cost could be millions of dollars lost to class action lawsuits.

When considering technology and security of information, review the types of information your business gathers and could potentially gather over the next five years and assign the appropriate level of risk for each type of information. There is a clear ranking system where your customers' personally-identifying information is of paramount importance. Business marketing or financial projections are in the bottom tier because if that information leaks, it is not that important to the survival of the business. However, exposing the personal information of hundreds or thousands of customers could destroy your business. There is a lot of grey in between these two examples, so it is important to consult an IT expert to review your technology set up.

First question: What kind of information do you have in your business and should you be worried about it?

If you think your company doesn't handle any sensitive information, think again. Personal information includes any data that could identify a specific person. If you store any of this information, you need to ensure you are doing so securely. Some examples include:

- Full name
- Email address
- Phone number
- Banking or credit card numbers
- Tax filing number
- Passport number
- Driver's license number

Second question: What are the policies around setting up new user accounts and how is the system protected from intrusion?

If you do plan to maintain your own server, here a few small pointers. When not in use, servers should be in sleep mode to conserve energy and a screensaver should come on after ten minutes of inactivity, for the security of the server. This will also help keep the system secure from unauthorized passersby. Requiring a password to unlock the server is a must-have security measure.

Third question: How do you implement those policies?

If it's at the implementation stage, that's when technology comes into play. If you have good policies, and you know the risk, the technology will follow. Binks shared this in an illustrative example:

A manager of a bustling manufacturing and retail store was determined that they would never move to the cloud. They didn't trust cloud security. I asked, "Where's your server?" and he led me down the hall to show me. We walked into a room with an open door and the server was standing there on a rack. There was zero security. Literally anyone could've walked in and damaged or taken it. It was also not configured properly, so it could have easily been hacked. How secure is that? Sure, it's secure in that he can see it, but not secure compared to a data centre. A data centre has all kinds of security that reduces risks by at least a factor of ten.

Your highly sensitive personal information is far more physically secure in a data centre than in your office. Corporate data centres are high security; they have security guards, surveillance, restricted access to the building. Trying to get into one would be like breaking into Fort Knox. They are also not vulnerable to extreme weather in the same way that a warehouse is. It's unlikely to suffer accidental water damage from roof leaks because there are alarms and checks in place. Amazon Web Services takes security so seriously they do not allow employees to tour the buildings like they do with fulfillment warehouses, just in case.

However, the physical location of the server is not the most important element of digital storage. There needs to be a digital blanket surrounding your firm's data, and if that doesn't exist, it doesn't matter where your server is located. The information is vulnerable to hacking unless it is encrypted and access to the data is restricted to specified authenticated users. Encryption is like an intangible lock-and-key to your digital information. This encryption and digital security is paramount for cloud solutions because they can't exist without it. The folks who run data storage make security their top priority because they can dedicate their entire working day to run it well. When you are also doing the fourteen other roles in your business, it's unlikely you will know how to best install computer hardware, unless you have a great IT professional to help.

The Equifax information leak in 2017 was a huge scandal because they did not inform their users in a timely or appropriate manner. The information that was hacked contained personally-identifying information, which makes their users vulnerable to identity theft. Equifax has a legal duty to keep that information safe and to inform users of any breaches. Your business has this responsibility too, if you collect and store this type of information. For the average small business, this is a lot of responsibility and a lot of risk. It would be better to outsource this to an online system instead, which would be better equipped to tackle this responsibility.

While security from hackers is the main risk from a legal perspective, you must also consider the risk of hardware failure. Planning against this type of failure is called redundancy. Redundancy is critical to managing your data so that you don't suddenly lose all your records one day because your hardware died. Cloud systems are built to be redundant. While using the cloud doesn't mean you shouldn't have your records backed up, it does mean that if that hard drive suddenly dies, you haven't lost everything. Similarly, when updates happen, they are staggered among the data centres' machines, so you don't experience any downtime. This means you always automatically have the most up-to-date software that ensures tip-top security.

In addition to being redundant, being off-site is also a value add. Let's say you have an office with both in-person and remote employees (like sales people who submit orders from client sites). You have a local server that lives in the office headquarters and head office loses power. Now no one at the office can work due to lack of power. But also anyone outside the office can't access the server and doesn't know why the connection is failing, so they're twiddling their thumbs waiting to find out what's happening. If your data was on the cloud, they could continue working because your headquarters losing power has no impact on your remote workers' ability to connect to your company data systems.

If you wanted to install this yourself, to replicate the same level of redundancy Amazon offers, this is what you would need to do:

- Multiple physical hard drives in a machine, to ensure adequate backup to prevent the loss of data within that machine
- Three machines that are copies of each other located in different areas within the region, far enough apart that a natural disaster or power grid failure would not affect more than one at a time
- A redundant array of independent disks (RAID) configuration
- Plus all the networking and automation to keep all the machines and hard drives in sync at all times

However, if you use a cloud service, it's included in your monthly fee.

The Eco-Friendly Benefits

Back to Binks' general rule: the eco-friendly option for a small business is to leverage online data storage. Hopefully, we have convinced you that moving to online data storage is a great idea due to its many other additional benefits outlined above. It's also great for the environment.

Data centres are more energy efficient than running your own personal server because they use capacity appropriately. Most small business local servers run 24 hours a day, like a data centre, but they only use about 10% of the server's capacity. By contrast, a data centre will typically use 70-80% of the capacity of its data units. An individual, local server uses the same amount of power as a data centre, but a data centre is utilizing that energy more efficiently. The utilization is, therefore, more efficient from a data centre. A data centre will always leave 20% of the server unused in case of bursts in activity. This allows those using the data centre to always access their data seamlessly.

Plus, if your data is stored in data centres owned by Google or Amazon, they've already committed to making their servers carbon neutral, so you know that your necessary backups are going into a carbon neutral cloud opposed to one that traps greenhouse gases.

An additional energy-saving tip is to turn off computers at the end of the day. This saves energy overnight, and the computers can go through any updates if necessary and save power while no one is in the office.

In Practice: Technology Through Generations

My grandfather started his accounting firm in approximately 1952, and my dad started working in the family business at age fourteen. I followed in my father's footsteps and worked for Richardsons Taxation Services in my childhood. My family has generations of experience managing entirely too much paperwork, so it stands to reason that we have encountered some of its pitfalls along the way. My dad tells a story about my grandfather that underscores just how fragile a physical paperwork system is, in ways that can be hard to predict:

> On this particular day in 1957, [grand]dad was belting along on a gravel road near Banana when he hit a very bad patch and promptly lost control of the car. The Austin A90 rolled four times. His assistant was lucky to stay in the car. The boot flew open and all the files, papers, and records were scattered all over the bush. The windscreen fell out in one piece, and [grand]dad flew out after it. He ended up lying on his back on the road, the car beside him teetering—thankfully, it fell back on its wheels. Neither of them were seriously hurt, and they managed to pick up all the files and records from around the bush. They were never sure if they got everything, but they never noticed anything missing.

Can you imagine how devastating it would've been if it was raining? That paperwork, scattered across the Outback, lost forever. The potential cost to my grandfather's business is hard to quantify, but he certainly would have needed to re-do all the lost paperwork, at a minimum. If a client had been audited and the paperwork was missing, that would have been doubly devastating and unnecessarily stressful.

I have very clear memories of afternoons spent, alongside my brother, cleaning out the warehouse where these client records were kept. Given the firm kept paper records for half a century, I'm not exaggerating when I say 'warehouse'. As someone with a dust allergy, sifting through dusty boxes to find old client records that could be destroyed was not a pleasant way to spend every summer of my teen years.

In 2005, my dad implemented a new electronic filing system and switched printing his copy of a tax return from single-sided to double-sided and half-sized, to fit a total of four pages on a single sheet of paper. This dramatically reduced how much paper needed to be stored, up to 75% reduction for each return. This means less paper to sort through in that dusty warehouse in more recent years, which everyone appreciates.

One of the biggest factors for paper reduction this millennium has been backing up year-end documents for every business electronically instead of printing them. For some clients, the combination of Income Statement, General Ledger, Trial Balance, and Balance Sheet for the whole year could be a mountain of paper. Now, it's easy to pull all client records going back to 2005 without going to search in the warehouse.

While my dad hasn't moved entirely to the cloud, he does recognize the importance of technology and has a local server. He also encourages his clients to use online record-keeping rather than sending him a box of receipts. However, this doesn't save his server from the annual cyclone season that blows through North Queensland. Recently, in preparing for a severe tropical cyclone, the server was incorrectly stored in the safe and damaged as a result. Luckily, he had offsite backups but repairs to the server took many days. During this time, his staff could not work effectively because the electronic filing system requires server access. Both the server repairs and lost productivity were very expensive.

Luckily, when I started my accounting practice, the cloud was readily available. I've been conscious to avoid creating and maintaining physical copies of client files. With e-sign software, I no longer even need clients to sign a printed copy of their tax returns. Compared to my dad's warehouse, the paperwork I keep fits within a small filing cabinet. Not only does this mean my storage costs are low, but also my records are safe from fire, flood, theft, and cyclone damage.

To store my client data in paper the same way my father does would cost me at least $1,200 per year on self-storage alone, which does not guarantee against physical damage and has very limited security against theft. By going digital, I have no need to buy paper and ink for a printer, an estimated savings of $100 annually. Additionally, it makes hiring easier since my employees just need to be authorized on my cloud system and can work from home instead of having to come to an office. This is a great perk for them and a reduction in office space cost for me. Comparing the estimated $1,300 annual cost of storing papers to the $220 annual software fees, I'm coming out ahead even without factoring in office space cost, nor the value the cloud adds in data security, environmental benefits, and the ability to work remotely.

Encouraging Tech Literacy

The benefits of upgrading your technology can facilitate time and resource savings, creating efficiencies by automating a tedious manual process that can free your staff to do more important things, like your sustainability audit.

It is important to dedicate adequate time and resources to train staff on technology that they use in their day-to-day lives. It's also important to give your tech support the authority and capability to implement the most efficient IT system so your business can fully leverage technology to its advantage. Browsing through any tech forum, such as Tales from Tech Support, will reveal a number of tech inefficiencies that waste physical resources and staff time. For example, instead of a staff member saving a document to PDF through the built in option to 'Save to PDF' available on all computers, and saving documents to the computer's drive in order to attach them to an email, there are multiple accounts of folks printing out the document and scanning it as a PDF to send as an email, then trashing the printed copy.

There are multiple issues with this.

1. **Wasted resources:** The printed documented has a life that was entirely unnecessary. Money was wasted on that paper and the electricity to run the printer.

2. **Staff time:** Instead of spending twenty seconds to save the document to the computer and then attaching it to an email, the staff had to print, wait for the printout, scan the document, make sure it scanned properly, then create the email and attach the scanned document. Depending on the size of the document, this would take at least five minutes for a small document and upwards of ten minutes for a very large one.

3. **Low-quality final product:** Any scan will lose quality compared to the original. If there are any issues with your scanner such as misalignments or extra lines scanning into the page, then the scanned document will be distorted and pixelated. It looks unprofessional. If the recipient can't read it properly due to the pixelation, that could lead to more problems and wasted staff time. I once had an issue paying a client's new staff member because I received a pixelated account information sheet that made a zero look like an eight. Two days later, when the payment bounced back, I spent an extra hour with the bank and staff member to uncover the issue. This wouldn't have happened if I'd received the original document in the first place.

4. **Productivity loss:** These extra five to ten minutes of technical inefficiencies add up. It's unlikely that your staff enjoy the process of scanning and filing when they could be doing more of the jobs that interest them. Jobs that could be making your customers happier,

your products better, or your processes faster. This is a hidden cost to your business as staff are demotivated by tasks they feel are tedious. Tedious tasks are a symptom of a bigger problem: rampant business inefficiencies.

All of these costs add up. It would, therefore, be a great investment for your business to hire an IT professional to make sure your systems are working as efficiently as possible, and implementing changes to improve what isn't working.

In Practice: Phil

Phil is a full-service agency focused on helping philanthropic organizations and mission-driven businesses. Their entire business is cloud-based, from their workflow to payroll to client communications. Their filing system resides on Google Drive, where the team can access any file at any time, from anywhere. Never again will they be in a client meeting and realize they've forgotten something important. They can just pull it up on Google Drive in seconds. All their projects and inter-company communications are managed via Monday.com, which helps keep them organized, on track, and able to connect with each other instantly within office hours, no matter where they are located. Vyte is among their preferred scheduling software options, and can schedule phone calls, in-person meetings, or video conferences. Staff are paid via direct deposit, through the payroll software Nethris. Phil has every aspect of their business covered so they can focus on serving their clients to make a bigger difference in the world. In utilizing these different software packages, Phil has successfully leveraged technology to its fullest extent.

Fourteen

Bigger Steps

Switch to a Credit Union

If you have not already done this, I highly recommend moving your business accounts out of a major bank. Major banks were embroiled in scandals long before the 2008 global financial crisis including creating new accounts you didn't authorize to charge extra fees, authorizing loans that you can't afford, and financing projects that are damaging to communities and the environment. Due to their size, big banks tend to have access to a lot of money, and they can invest it in many ethically questionable ways. You can dive into the details about your bank on BankTrack. Some dodgy deals could be related to experimenting on animals, like the bank deal between Chase Bank, JP Morgan, and La Roche, where a number of banks funded a project that led to experiments on chimpanzees. Others help with building oil pipelines that destroy forests and negatively impact rural settlements, especially when there are spills. These deals would not have been funded without cash. Your local credit union would not fund these kinds of projects, mostly because they primarily invest in their local communities and local businesses.

Credit unions are an important part of keeping money local. Rather than your money helping a big bank make money that pays their CEO exorbitant amounts, and only helping out a local business if they meet a very stringent set of criteria, a credit union wants to invest in businesses like yours.

Now, I know what you're thinking. "It's going to be such a pain in the arse to switch to a new bank! I have my credit cards and automatic bills set up. This will be so hard!"

I know this because I've been there. I procrastinated about opening an account with a local credit union for almost a year before I finally booked the appointment to open the account. And that's when I realized I'd fallen into the oldest financial trap: building it up to be a bigger deal than it was. With most challenges like this, psychology was actually the barrier to creating an account, not the actual process. Once I'd finally picked up the phone to make the appointment, I was in their office less than a week later with some basic paperwork, getting my account set up. Once it was set up, I received an email with the directions to set up my online banking account, and I could begin using my new credit union account. I didn't switch everything to the new account immediately, as that would have been quite overwhelming. But over time, I gradually used my credit union account for more and more of my business needs. First, it was to receive payments so that all my receivables went into that account. As needed, I transferred money out to my other banks to pay off credit cards and pay bills until I had the chance to switch to paying them through the credit union over the following months.

Become a B Corporation

This is the penultimate way for businesses to legitimately brand themselves as sustainable. Like Fair Trade is the standard for ethical coffee, this is the standard for ethical businesses. It is not for the faint of heart, however, as their assessment of a company takes into account each situation and assigns points for business practices in line with transparency, good governance, supporting employees, protecting the environment, and so on. Depending on your industry, how many employees you have, if you sell products or make products, each of these variables can be taken into account and be balanced to ensure your company meets or incorporates a best practice standard while being flexible for the many different forms a small business may take.

The critical importance of a B Corporation in North America is to embed sustainable, ethical values into a company's incorporation articles. As previously mentioned, in the U.S., a business is legally required to generate profit, sometimes at the expense of everything else. However, successful companies have been founded and made widely profitable defying this legal mandate. But when the founder sells their business, the new owners can ignore the founding principles. If the business mandate and articles don't reflect ethical business practices, there is nothing forcing the new owners to stay true to the ethics that brought the company success. Several companies have gone from growing and profitable to failing merely because of the ethical mismanagement of new owners.

Hence, owners can ensure their companies continue to be a force for good, now and in the future, by becoming B Corp certified. This protects the company's founding principles by law, particularly important in the U.S., but also forces small businesses to articulate and write down their company's ideology. If a business only purchases from sustainably-verified suppliers, but it isn't written down, then it becomes harder to enforce as the company grows. Publication on their website also brings a measure of transparency and accountability.

The idea behind a B Corp is to solidify and measure the sustainable efforts of a company. This is often hard to do, and the bar is constantly being raised. They also want to teach you and your company about best practices and ways you can implement them in your business decisions. Ideally, you will come out of the B Corp assessment with more questions than when you went in. This assessment will allow reflection into your company, to see where you could be improving or where you are already outperforming others.

Strong EcoLabels

If your business makes consumer goods, particularly food-related goods, an important bigger step for your company is investing in EcoLabels, if you aren't already. This includes going through the process of verifying that your product is organic, cruelty-free, and responsibly and sustainably sourced. These EcoLabels and standards are important and protect not only consumers, but industry integrity as well. Companies claiming to be sustainable but unwilling to go through an EcoLabel process is usually where consumers smell greenwashing. They provide a level of certainty that a set of standard practices are being met.

Some of the EcoLabels currently available are:
- GMO Free
- USDA Certified Organic
- Forest Stewardship Council (FSC) for responsibly sourced paper products
- Marine stewardship council (MSC), the equivalent of the FSC for marine products

There are also EcoLabels for country-specific regions. This area would require more in-depth research to decide what makes the most sense for your company.

Learning from Sustainable Giants

We aren't alone in our green pursuits, so we can easily find mentors and examples to inspire us to do better. Here are a few thoughts to motivate you:

1. There are a number of multi-million and billion-dollar companies that are successful, sustainable, and eco-friendly. How do they use innovation to build such an empire?
2. Purpose-driven profit is at the centre of green giants' success, and they were able to normalize and popularize their brand through good marketing and competitive pricing.
3. Use strategies to target the causally green consumer to buy a product/service over a less ethical competitor.

There are a growing number of billion-dollar multinationals that are successful and profitable *because* they embedded sustainability into every facet of their business from day one. Unilever, The Body Shop, and Danone are excellent examples of this, as they reject practices that do not stand up to good governance principles or long-term environmental protections. On the financial reporting side, for example, Unilever abolished the practice of releasing quarterly reports as CEO Paul Polman found these created too much focus on short-term profit generation and hindered the application of projects that needed long-term investment. He says it has helped lead to a 300% growth of Unilever over his ten-year tenure since implementing this commitment to focus on the long-term.

Tesla Inc. is an interesting company to learn from because they are the largest and, arguably, the most successful electric car manufacturer. Tesla didn't get to this point by focusing on the environmental benefits of their cars. They appealed to their buyer's baser instincts: prestige, vanity, and showing off to peers. Their cars look like other luxury vehicles and are very expensive. You know anyone driving a Tesla is rich because their price range is not within most people's budgets. Yet Tesla continues to sell more cars year after year, and its business continues to expand. The cars were designed to appeal to what car enthusiasts love about cars. This is the same reason Hero Burger focuses on being a tasty burger, rather than on its sustainable supply chain.

In contrast, Whole Foods Market's entire brand and marketing focus has been on their environment-conscious, organic produce. They were the first grocer in the United States to become USDA Certified Organic. From their beginnings in the 1980s, they were committed to doing things differently. Their brand only grew as more consumers wanted to access a variety of organic produce, as this is a core selling point for their business.

All of these companies are also heavily involved in political lobbying for tax breaks, incentives, or regulation changes that benefit their companies. Lobbying government officials to enact regulations that raise the bar on sustainable standards is an excellent way your company can go further and create ripple effects with your impact. These efforts could take many forms, but you can start with something simple like partnering with your local government to plant more trees in public spaces. Or it could be lobbying or collaborating with other businesses to support a local compost program to divert food waste from landfills and decrease your community's greenhouse emissions. It might look like lobbying your local or state government to ban plastics that can't be recycled or composted in your area. You could encourage your local council to include mandatory green spaces and art installations when developing or building a new mall or suburb. Or maybe it's working with your local library and schools to install TerraCycle recycling bins for the entire community. There are endless possibilities.

Fifteen

The Conclusion, but Not the End

Are you overwhelmed now? Is your brain flowing with ideas? Are you excited by the possibility of revolutionizing your business while saving the world? Don't let the momentum die. Start now by writing down ideas, sharing them with your business colleagues, and creating an action plan. Don't let this drop to the bottom of your to-do list. Also, put a note in your calendar to revisit parts of the book that you aren't ready to address. Remember, this journey won't happen in a day. It is important to make continual, consistent progress. Climate change is something that we all, including myself, distance ourselves from. We who are lucky enough to live in houses, have electricity readily available, water at the turn of a tap—we don't see, nor do we want to acknowledge, our role in climate change.

I've always cared about the environment and wanted to do my best to protect it and encourage others to do the same, but I realized how desperately the earth needed my attention when I saw time-lapse photos of the changes happening to the earth. Truly, you can't appreciate or intimately understand the destruction we've inflicted on our planet until you see the visual impact.

Looking through these time lapses showed me that I needed to act. Immediately. This book was the end result. If we continue to do nothing, we are marching ourselves towards doom. But with change, we can change our fate.

Climate change shifts energy costs and consumer behaviour, all of which impact the success of your business. The reality is that we live in a world facing unprecedented change, but this creates extraordinary opportunities. Preparing for these opportunities, anticipating what changes will come and

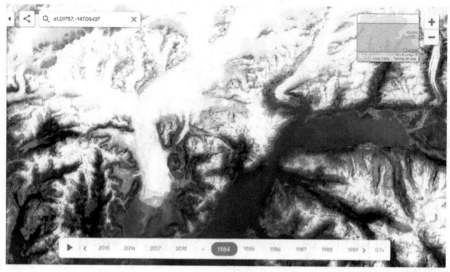

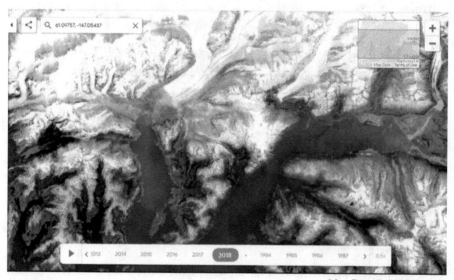

Figure 6 Columbia Glacier Retreat, Alaska USA, 1984 and 2018 satellite images

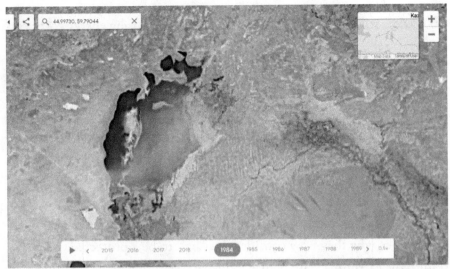

Map Data © 2019 Google

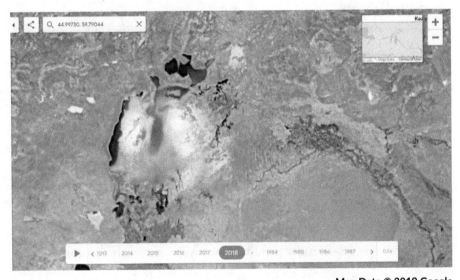

Map Data © 2019 Google

Figure 7 Drying of the aral sea, Kazakhstan and Uzbekistan, 1984 and 2018 satellite images

You can explore other areas of the world further at Google's Earth Timelapse Engine: earthengine.google.com/timelapse

are needed, will be key to sustaining your business. Rising energy costs, carbon taxes, and increased environmental regulations are already impacting businesses around the world. By reducing your expense on energy and natural resources, your business will reduce exposure to the uncertainty of fluctuating prices and regulations.

The future will have more rules and regulations to protect the environment, and it will be far more costly to be inefficient towards our natural resources. In Bolivia, the earth is protected by law because of their history of oil disasters that have destroyed vast amounts of natural resources. This had huge ongoing costs to their economy, health care, and restoration efforts, hence why they now consider the earth to be a protected entity. To restore the earth to a state before industry began to destroy it would cost more than all the profits that have been made by the manufacturing industry in all of history.

You do have the ability to make changes. Small things, like bringing a travel mug when you go out for coffee, add up to make a larger impact. It also sets your frame of mind for larger projects like eco-friendly renovations, energy audits, and major purchases. And do it with your uniqueness and the guile that started your business!

It's easy to shrug our shoulders and say the problems are too large, lobbies and interest groups are too powerful, and the situation is too far out of our control. This isn't the case. We've made bigger changes than this for the betterment of the human race, and we can do it again.

We like living and shopping the way we do, even patting ourselves on the back for our eco-friendly products, but we're currently too comfortable with how we're living. We think we can go on like this, that structures put in place centuries ago can carry us into an ever-improving future. Evidence shows that the past can no longer be a template for our future.

So go forth more sustainably. Make some noise about the changes you want to see in your business and in your community. Advocate for more than just profit as a measure for success. Ask questions in your local communities about what can be done to improve the planet. The climate crisis is upon us, so this is the time for all of us to rise up and do what we can for the planet—not just for ourselves and our future, but for everyone.

Checklists

Small Steps

- ☐ Pollution incident prevention
- ☐ Waste minimization and recycling
- ☐ Energy efficiency
- ☐ Water conservation
- ☐ Green procurement
- ☐ Green transport planning (biking, car share)
- ☐ Carbon offsetting

Huge Steps

- ☐ Cleaner production
- ☐ Renewable energy
- ☐ Industrial symbiosis
- ☐ Eco-building
- ☐ Eco-design
- ☐ Product service systems

Business Culture Change Tips

- ☐ Write an environmental policy to cement your organization's commitment to sustainability
- ☐ Keep the policy to one page
- ☐ Engage your staff and make them part of the solution
- ☐ Make appropriate financial commitments
- ☐ Set up staff committees to develop small steps of improvement
- ☐ Set up action teams for huge steps
- ☐ Implement simple incentive schemes
- ☐ Provide feedback to all staff, especially when gains are realized
- ☐ Match your tone to the company culture

Waste Minimization
- ☐ Set all printers and copiers to double-sided printing as a default
- ☐ Provide internal documents in electronic format and use electronic media for invitations and registration for meetings, conferences, etc.
- ☐ Place paper recycling bins in every office and a general waste bin at the end of each corridor
- ☐ Use overhead projections and PowerPoint rather than handouts and make presentations available online instead of hardcopies
- ☐ Plan food for meetings carefully and let other staff know if there are leftovers
- ☐ Keep tight control on ordering stationery
- ☐ Encourage staff to reuse folders, box files, etc.
- ☐ Use multi-use envelopes for internal mail and restrict supply so staff have to reuse them
- ☐ Discourage large reports
- ☐ Avoid disposable cutlery and crockery

Top Tips For Energy Efficiency
- ☐ Run a switch-it-off campaign
- ☐ Provide info and feedback to staff on energy consumption
- ☐ Purchase ENERGY STAR compliant or equivalent office equipment
- ☐ Upgrade all lighting to energy efficient models
- ☐ Downgrade level of lighting in non-critical areas
- ☐ Install auto lighting controls, particularly for windowless rooms
- ☐ Set heating controls to optimum temperature and ensure they remain there
- ☐ Install a smart thermostat (like Ecobee) that will monitor changing temperatures for you. Particular useful in spring and autumn
- ☐ Install a tea urn rather than individual kettles
- ☐ Unplug laptops and other portable equipment to stop power leaks

Transportation Top Tips

- ☐ Create a green travel plan
- ☐ Restrict parking access to encourage other forms of commuting
- ☐ Provide bike racks, lockers, and showers
- ☐ Negotiate with public transport providers to optimize routes
- ☐ Provide reimbursements for employees who use public transport
- ☐ Hire or purchase efficient vehicles
- ☐ Use alternative, low carbon fuels like ethanol
- ☐ Train staff on fuel efficient driving techniques
- ☐ Discourage unnecessary travel to teleconferencing and back-loading of freight
- ☐ Eliminate unauthorized travel
- ☐ Encourage telecommuting

Eco-friendly Checklist

Do you:

- ☐ Notice when the lights are on or off in the room when you enter or leave?
- ☐ Hear water running when the tap is on?
- ☐ Have an awareness of how warm or cold a room is?
- ☐ Know which recycling/compost/garbage bin your waste belongs in?
- ☐ Know where to drop batteries to be safely recycled?
- ☐ Turn down the heat and put on a sweater?
- ☐ Avoid keeping air conditioning so cold that employees must wear cardigans?
- ☐ Know the best part of winter is wearing a sweater and snuggling up while your heat isn't turned up to be hotter than the sun?
- ☐ Pick up batteries that you see on the ground?
- ☐ Pick up rubbish on the streets and put it in the bin?

Resources

Sustainable Resources

Ecological Footprint: Fifteen easy questions to estimate the land and water you need to support your lifestyle. Interesting comparisons against footprint impacts from other areas of the world. | **myfootprint.org**

The Natural Step: Various resources and inspiring global examples to serve as a helpful guide for companies, communities, and governments to move towards socially and economically sustainable paths. | **naturalstep.com**

National Cooperative Business Association (NCBA): This is the oldest, largest, and most diverse network of socially and environmentally responsible businesses that is U.S. based. Organized by Co-op America, participating companies use business as a tool for social change. They use CSR in how they source, manufacture, and market their products, as well as how they run their offices and factories. They are committed to employing extraordinary and innovative practices that benefit workers, communities, customers, and the environment. | **ncbaclusa.coop**

Business Alliance for Local Living Economics (BALLE): This international alliance of more than 50 independently operated local business networks has members dedicated to building local living economies with a vision of a sustainable global economy. They build long-term economic empowerment and prosperity through local business ownership, economic justice, cultural diversity, and environmental stewardship. | **livingeconomies.org**

Institute for Local Self-Reliance: Non-profit research and educational organization that provides technical assistance and information on environmentally-sound economic development strategies. | **ilsr.org**

Leadership in Energy and Environmental Design (LEED): usgbc.org

B Corporation: bcorporation.net

Renewable Energy Certificates (RECs): This is a great way to offset your energy usage if putting up your own solar panel system or wind turbine isn't an option. By doing this, you are helping to accelerate a green-powered grid, as the partnership exists to expand the use of and access to solar energy. | **energy.gov/eere/solar/national-community-solar-partnership**

Bullfrog Power: This is a service to offset your home or business's electricity. They ensure the energy put on the grid on your behalf is from clean, low-impact, renewable sources. | **bullfrogpower.com**

Cradle to Cradle: Reviews environmentally intelligent design of products with consideration for the entire lifecycle of ecologically safe and healthy materials. | **c2ccertified.com**

ENERGY STAR: Fifty categories of appliances and products that use less energy, save money, and help protect the environment. | **energystar.gov**

Forest Stewardship Council (FSC): They set standards for responsible forest management and certify products from specific woodlands. | **fsc.org**

Greenguard Certification: They approve various building, home, and office décor products with low volatile organic compounds. | **greenguard.org**

Green Seal: They provide standards and certification for diverse products, including paints, windows, alternative-fuel vehicles, and paper. | **greenseal.org**

Green Globe: This is the worldwide benchmark and certification program for the international travel and tourism industry. | **greenglobe.com**

Travel Green Wisconsin: Here is an example of a state-wide movement promoting sustainable travel, including various checklist criteria for greening and localizing travel-related businesses in Wisconsin. They are the first state to do so. | **travelgreenwisconsin.com**

Certified Organic: www.ams.usda.gov/NOP

Scientific Certification Systems: They certify ecologically preferred products or services like cabinetry, doors, flooring, and paints. | **scscertified.com**

Corporate Standard of Compassion for Animals: Certifies cosmetics, personal care products, and household products that are not tested on animals. | **leapingbunny.org**

Environmental Choice: Also known as the Canadian EcoLogo. It certifies products and services as environmentally responsible based on life cycle analysis of harmful emissions, recycled content, water use, energy efficiency, and other factors. | **greenterrafirma.com/EcoLogo.html**

European Eco-label: Identifies goods and services that meet strict scientific criteria for minimizing environmental impacts. | **www.ec.europa.eu/environment/ecolabel/index_en.htm**

Less Emissions: Less was born out of a need to give Canadians a way to offset their air-travel-related emissions. | **less.ca/en-ca/**

Marine Stewardship Council: msc.org

Ocean Wise Seafood: Overfishing is a monumental, global issue. Ocean Wise seafood is a conservation program that makes it easy for consumers to choose sustainable seafood for the long-term health of our oceans. The Ocean Wise symbol next to a seafood item is assurance of an ocean-friendly seafood choice. | **seafood.ocean.org**

Good Environmental Choice Australia: An Australian entity that identifies products and services that have smaller ecological footprints in comparison to competitors. |
ecolabelindex.com/ecolabel/good-environmental-choice-australia

Green Guard: Certifies low emission building materials and indoor products. | **greenguard.org**

Building Green: Certifies a wide range of building, renovation, and home furnishing products. | **buildinggreen.com**

Take Back Your Time Day: Oct. 24 is dedicated to the preservation of our family, health, community, and environment by redirecting hours to pastimes like sharing dinner with friends and family. | **takebackyourtime.org**

Green Money Journal: Educating and empowering individuals and businesses to make informed financial decisions through aligning their personal, corporate, and financial principles. | **greenmoney.com**

Sustainablebusiness.com: Provides global news and networking services to help green businesses grow. Rather than covering a slice of the industry, they offer a unique lens on the field as a whole, covering all sectors that impact sustainability such as renewable energy, efficiency, green building, green investing, and organics. | **sustainablebusiness.com**

Good Capital: Investment firm accelerating flow of capital to innovative ventures and initiatives that create sustainable solutions to society's most challenging problems. | **goodcapitalproject.com**

Social Venture Circle: Angel investors for entrepreneurial companies that enhance bioregional, cultural, economic health, and diversity. | **svcimpact.org**

Green Options: greenoptions.com.au

For additional resources, consider the following websites:
- **EnvironmentalLeader.com**
- **Greenbiz.com**
- **SustainableBusiness.com**
- **Treehugger.com**
- **Worldchanging.com**

These are a few key green, sustainable, and socially responsible business-focused associations:
- Business for Social Responsibility: **bsr.org**
- World Business Council for Sustainable Development: **wbcsd.org**
- Social Venture Network: **svn.org**
- The Natural Step: **naturalstep.org**
- The Pew Center on Climate Change: **pewclimate.org**

Bibliography

A. R. Ravishankara, S. S. (1993). *Atmospheric Lifetimes of Long-Lived Halogenated Species*. Science. Retrieved September 24, 2015

Amazon. (2019). *Data Protection in Amazon S3*. Retrieved from Amazon Web Services: https://docs.aws.amazon.com/AmazonS3/latest/dev/DataDurability.html

Amazon. (2019). *Our Controls*. Retrieved from Amazon Web Services: https://aws.amazon.com/compliance/data-center/controls/

Bachman, G. (2009). *The Green Business Guide: A One Stop Resource for Businesses of All Shapes and Sizes to Implement Eco-friendly Policies, Programs, and Practices*. Career Press.

Bank Track. (2016). *Dodgy Deal by United States*. Retrieved from Bank Track: https://www.banktrack.org/search#category=banks&country=United%20States

Bank Tracks. (2015). *Patents on chimpanzees and other animals*. Retrieved from Bank Tracks Dodgy Deals: https://www.banktrack.org/project/patents_on_chimpanzees#popover=financiers

Beauchesne, S. (2017, October 20). Success Story: Beau's Brewery. (S. Richardson, Interviewer)

BDC. (n.d.). *10 things you (probably) didn't know about Canadian SMEs*. Retrieved from https://www.bdc.ca/en/articles-tools/business-strategy-planning/manage-business/pages/10-things-didnt-know-canadian-sme.aspx

Binks, G. (2017, May 30). Sustainable Tech for Small Businesses. (S. Richardson, Interviewer)

Boushey, H., & Glynn, S. (2012). *There Are Significant Business Costs to Replacing Employees*. Center for American Progress. Retrieved from https://www.scribd.com/document/112707536/There-Are-Significant-Business-Costs-to-Replacing-Employees

Buech, J. (2018, April 11). *The Rising Popularity of Fermented Drinks*. Retrieved July 28, 2018, from Mintel Blog: https://www.mintel.com/blog/drink-market-news/the-rising-popularity-of-fermented-drinks

Carson, R. (1962). *Silent Spring*. Houghton Mifflin.

CBC News. (2015, May 12). *Toronto condo goes green, cuts garbage to 1 bin a month*. Retrieved from CBC News: https://www.cbc.ca/news/canada/toronto/toronto-condo-goes-green-cuts-garbage-to-1-bin-a-month-1.3071758

Centre for Social Innovation. (2016). *CSI Community Bond*. Retrieved from Impact Investing: https://impactinvesting.ca/guidebook/case-studies/csi-community-bond/

Daniel, A.-M., Johnson, L., & Doucette, J. (2014). *Greening Your Office: The Environmentally Friendly Way*. Self-Counsel Press.

Department of Energy. (2011). *17 billion tons CO2 every year: 51% of a households gas emissions*. Retrieved October 7, 2018, from United States Department of Energy: http://www.energy.gov/sciencetech/carbonsequestration.htm

Encyclopedia.com. (2019, October 30). The Body Shop International plc. Retrieved from Encyclopedia.com: https://www.encyclopedia.com/social-sciences-and-law/economics-business-and-labor/businesses-and-occupations/body-shop-international-plc

Environmental Protection Agency. (2008). *Facts and Figures for 2008*. Retrieved from Municipal Solid Waste Generation, Recycling, and Disposal in the U.S.

Estes, J. (2009). *Smart Green: How to Implement Sustainable Business Practices in Any Industry and Make Money*. Wiley.

Esty, D. C., & Winston, A. S. (2006). *Green to Gold: How Smart Companies Use Environmental Strategy to Innovate, Create Value, and Build Competitive Advantage*. Brilliance Audio.

Fink, L. (2016). *Larry Fink's 2016 Letter to CEOs*. Retrieved from BlackRock: https://www.blackrock.com/corporate/investor-relations/2016-larry-fink-ceo-letter

First Carbon Solutions. (2016, May). *Top Myths about Sustainability*. Retrieved from First Carbon Solutions: https://www.firstcarbonsolutions.com/resources/newsletters/may-2016-top-myths-about-sustainability/top-myths-about-sustainability/

Friend, G. (2009). *The Truth About Green Business*. Upper Saddle River: Que Publishing.

Fuller, K. (2017, August 28). In Practice: Phil. (S. Richardson, Interviewer)

Gelski, J. (2019, October 1). *Sustainable product market could hit $150 billion in U.S. by 2021*. Food Business News, 1. Retrieved November 9, 2019, from https://www.foodbusinessnews.net/articles/13133-sustainable-product-market-could-hit-150-billion-in-us-by-2021

Gifford, M. (2017, August 29). Open Concept B Corp Certification. (S. Richardson, Interviewer)

Goodall, C., & Bullock, H. (2009). *The Green Guide For Business: The Ultimate Environment Handbook for Businesses of All Sizes*. Profile Books.

Greenhouse Gas Protocol. (2013). *Required Greenhouse Gases in Inventories. World Resources Institute and World Business Council for Sustainable Development*. Retrieved from https://ghgprotocol.org/sites/default/files/standards_supporting/Required gases and GWP values.pdf

Hanson, G. N. (n.d.). *Bicycling in Muenster, Germany*. Retrieved from State University of New York at Stony Brook Department of Geosciences: http://www.geo.sunysb.edu/bicycle-muenster/index.html

Hardwick, M. (2018, October 15). *6 Tips to Reduce Office Plug Loads*. Retrieved from TrickleStar Blog: https://blog.tricklestar.com/6-tips-to-reduce-office-plug-loads

Hardwick, M. (2018, April 2). *How Much Energy Does a Computer Workstation Use?* Retrieved from TrickleStar Blog: https://blog.tricklestar.com/how-much-energy-does-a-computer-use

Henderson, H., Long, L., & Nash, T. (2017). *2017 Green Transition Scoreboard® Report*. Toronto: Ethical Markets Media. Retrieved April 2017

Hitchcock, D. (2006). The Business Guide to Sustainability: Practical Strategies and Tools for Organizations. Routledge.

Hoar, B. (2016). Strategies for a sustainable office. (S. Richardson, Interviewer)

Ivanko, J. D., & Kivirist, L. (2008). *Ecopreneuring: Putting Purpose and the Planet Before Profits*. New Society Publishers.

Jia, F., Gosling, J., & Witzel, M. (2019). *CHINA EDITION - Sustainable Champions: How International Companies are Changing the Face of Business in China.* Routledge. Retrieved Nov 28, 2019

Jordan, C. (2007, July 23). *Running the Numbers.* Retrieved from The Morning News: https://themorningnews.org/gallery/running-the-numbers

Kala, M. (2010, March 29). *How much does a sheet of paper weigh?* Retrieved from Ansuz People Before Tribes: https://ansuz.sooke.bc.ca/entry/12

Kane, G. (2010). *The Three Secrets of Green Business.* London: Earthscan.

Kaplan, J. (2009). *Greening Your Small Business: How to Improve Your Bottom Line, Grow Your Brand, Satisfy Your Customers - and Save the Planet.* Prentice Hall Press.

Leung, D. a. (2011, June). *The Contribution of Small and Medium-sized Businesses to Gross Domestic Product: A Canada–United States Comparison.* Retrieved from Statistics Canada: Economic Analysis Division: https://www.conferenceboard.ca/sme/default.aspx

Lou, Y., & Zhu, W. (2007, May 16). *PetroChina fees Sudan heat as fidelity sells shares.* International Herald Tribune.

Lütke, T. (2019, September 12). *We need to talk about carbon: Shopify commits a minimum of $5M annually to fight for the environment with the Shopify Sustainability Fund.* Retrieved from Shopify: https://news.shopify.com/we-need-to-talk-about-carbon#

Madu, C. N. (2012). *Handbook of Sustainability Management.* World Scientific. Retrieved Nov 28, 2019

Marshall, J. (1996). *PG&E to Pay $333 Million In Pollution Suit.* SFGate, 1.

McDonough, W., & Braungart, M. (2002). *Cradle to Cradle: Remaking the Way We Make Things.* North Point Press.

Morningstar Analyst Rating. (2019, March 20). *Parnassus Endeavor Institutional.* Retrieved from Morningstar: https://www.morningstar.com/funds/xnas/pfpwx/quote

Mintzer, R. (2009). *Start Your Own Green Business: Your Step-By-Step Guide to Success.* Entrepreneur Press.

Mueller-Glodde, T. U. (2017, April 8). Collaborative Workshops. (S. Richardson, Interviewer)

National Oceanic and Atmospheric Administration. (2018). *Billions*. Retrieved from National Centres for Environmental Information: https://www.ncdc.noaa.gov/billions/

Olson, E. G. (2009). *Better Green Business: Handbook for Environmentally Responsible and Profitable Business Practices*. FT Press.

Parisi, P. (2017, October 17). *The power of partnerships: Why businesses are better together*. The Globe and Mail, 1. Retrieved from https://www.theglobeandmail.com/report-on-business/careers/leadership-lab/the-power-of-partnerships-why-businesses-are-better-together/article36529258/

PBS. (2013, March 3). *Protecting Americans From Danger in the Drinking Water*. Retrieved from PBS Newshour: https://www.pbs.org/video/pbs-newshour-protecting-americans-from-danger-in-the-drinking-water/

Peters, A. (2019, February 14). *Most millennials would take a pay cut to work at a environmentally responsible company*. Fast Company, 1. Retrieved November 24, 2019, from https://www.fastcompany.com/90306556/most-millennials-would-take-a-pay-cut-to-work-at-a-sustainable-company

Pierre-Louis, K. (2012). *Green Washed: Why We Can't Buy Our Way to a Green Planet*. Ig Publishing.

Porritt, J. (2006). *Capitalism as If the World Matters*. Earthscan Publications.

Puma. (2011). *Clever Little Report*. Munich. Retrieved from https://about.puma.com/-/media/files/pdf/investor-relations/ar_2011.ashx

Resource Nation. (2015). *Computer Settings*. Retrieved from Resource Nation Blog: http://www.resourcenation.com

Richardson, D. (2016). Cost of Transporting Empty Trucks. (S. Richardson, Interviewer)

Sanford, C., & Henderson, R. (2011). *The Responsible Business: Reimagining Sustainability and Success*. Jossey-Bass.

Somerville, M. (2014). *All You Need Is Less: The Eco-friendly Guide to Guilt-Free Green Living and Stress-Free Simplicity*. Viva Editions.

Steffen, A. (2011). *Worldchanging, Revised Edition: A User's Guide for the 21st Century*. Harry N. Abrams.

Stein, C. (2017, April 20). Beekeeper's Naturals Origins. (S. Richardson, Interviewer)

Strauss, S. D. (2013). *The World Entrepreneurship Forum's Guide to Planet Entrepreneur: Secrets to Succeeding in the Global Marketplace*. John Wiley & Sons.

Suzuki, D., & Boyd, D. R. (2009). *David Suzuku's Green Guide*. Greystone Books.

Taylor, B. (2016). EnviroStewards Philosophy. (S. Richardson, Interviewer)

The Atmosphere Fund. (2019). *A Clearer View on Ontario's Emissions. Toronto: City of Toronto & Province of Ontario*. Retrieved from https://www.opg.com/document/greenhouse-gas-emissions-associated-with-various-methods-of-power-generation-in-ontario

Thomas, R. (2019, October 16). ESG's in 401K's. (S. Richardson, Interviewer)

United States Environmental Protection Agency. (1991). *Indoor Air Facts No. 4 Sick Building Syndrome*. Retrieved November 22, 2019, from https://www.epa.gov/sites/production/files/2014-08/documents/sick_building_factsheet.pdf

Various. (2019). *Animal Testing*. Retrieved November 26, 2019, from Wikipedia: https://en.wikipedia.org/wiki/Animal_testing

Vasil, A. (2007). *Ecoholic: Your Guide to the Most Environmentally Friendly Information, Products and Services in Canada*. Toronto: Vintage Canada.

Wilcox, M. (2017, February 28). *L'Oreal, Chanel and Nespresso pioneer 'carbon insetting'*. Retrieved May 6, 2017, from GreenBiz Group: https://www.greenbiz.com/article/loreal-chanel-and-nespresso-pioneer-carbon-insetting

Wilhelm, K. (2013). *Return on Sustainability: How Business Can Increase Profitability and Address Climate Change in an Uncertain Economy*. FT Press.

Willard, B. (2012). *The New Sustainability Advantage: Seven Business Case Benefits of a Triple Bottom Line*. New Society Publishers.

Woods, D. (2017, February 23). *Perspectives Blog*. Retrieved May 6, 2017, from Energy Factor: https://energyfactor.exxonmobil.com/perspectives/the-future-of-energy-opportunities-and-challenges/

World Commission on Environment and Development, U. N. (1987). *Our Common Future*. Retrieved from Sustainable Development: https://sustainabledevelopment.un.org/content/documents/5987our-common-future.pdf

Yee, R., & Yee, T. (2019, October 21). ESG Screening of 401K. (S. Richardson, Interviewer)

Yoder, K. (2019, October 3). *Some economics nerds just realized how much climate change will cost us*. Retrieved from Grist: https://grist.org/article/some-economics-nerds-just-realized-how-much-climate-change-will-cost-us/

Index

About the Author

An accountant. A farm girl. An environmental professional. Sam Richardson
has melded her passion, personal life,
and profession to become an expert in
environmental finance. Her first book,
Ethical Profit, a book of practical advice
to decrease your environmental impact
while increasing profits, is the manifes-
tation of her expertise.

After graduating from Queensland
University of Technology with a Bachelor of Business, she followed the family tradition and became a third-generation accountant. She has worked in
the accounting field for over 15 years. Her desire to have a greater impact
on people and small businesses, led her to open up a small accounting outfit
where she became the first Canadian accountant to be a certified B Corp.
Outside of accounting, Richardson enjoys cycling, discovering new places,
reading and spending time with friends.

CPSIA information can be obtained
at www.ICGtesting.com
Printed in the USA
LVHW012041251219
641665LV00001B/2